Paul
Ballman

RED
PILL

The Truth About
Leadership

ISBN 978-1-911079-00-2

Acorn Independent Press

About The Author

Paul Ballman has a long history of consulting to the most senior leaders in the world's largest companies. Following his degree at The London School of Economics, he completed a Doctorate in Psychology at Birkbeck College, University of London. He began his career in Telecommunications at Nortel Networks before moving into the world of business consulting, firstly at Roffey Park Management, and then at RHR International. In 1998, he co-founded The Development Alliance before joining YSC later the same year. During his 17 years at YSC, he set up their online business, opened the Sydney office, oversaw the development of the Asia Pacific region, and eventually assumed responsibility for all 17 global offices, becoming co-CEO in 2013. Throughout this time, he acted as an assessor, coach and consultant to the top levels of a range of clients across sectors including Financial Services, FMCG, Retail, Pharmaceuticals and Mining. Following Private Equity investment into the business, Paul has returned to Telecommunications and joined Vodafone UK in 2015.

To find out more visit: ***redpill-leadership.com***

Acknowledgements

This book would not have been possible without the support of a range of wonderful people. In particular, I would like to thank those people who read chapters and provided useful feedback. Rob Morris, Angela David, Elisa Krantz, Ella Oancea and John Forrest, your support and encouragement have meant the world to me. I have also been lucky enough to have received introductions, coaching, and advice and guidance from Stephen Page. Thank you. The support of my employers has been invaluable; firstly at YSC and then Vodafone. In the latter case, a special thank you goes to Daniel Cloke who provided a stimulating yet flexible working environment that added impetus to the later chapters. Thanks also to Leila Dewji and Ali Dewji at Acorn Independent Press and Helen Lewis at Literally PR for their support in getting this book to market. Finally, I would like to acknowledge my wife, Rajinder, and sons, Adam and Arran, who have tolerated the many hours that I have spent at home, absorbed in the endeavour.

For Rajinder, Adam and Arran

I met a traveller from an antique land
Who said: "Two vast and trunkless legs of stone
Stand in the desert. Near them, on the sand,
Half sunk, a shattered visage lies, whose frown,
And wrinkled lip, and sneer of cold command,
Tell that its sculptor well those passions read
Which yet survive, stamped on these lifeless things,
The hand that mocked them and the heart that fed:
And on the pedestal these words appear:
`My name is Ozymandias, king of kings:
Look on my works, ye Mighty, and despair!'
Nothing beside remains. Round the decay
Of that colossal wreck, boundless and bare
The lone and level sands stretch far away."

Percy Bysshe Shelley

Contents

Introduction
The Panacea Problem

"Here comes the wise man in the story of sick times,
telling you how to find the passage of satisfaction."
A. F. Moritz

It is the 25th of June 1993 in a market town in the South East of England, and a group of engineers are gathering in a conference centre. They belong to the now departed Nortel telecommunications company, and they spend their lives working at the cutting edge of fibre optics and experimenting with the video-telephony of the future. The group is predominantly white, male and super geeky. In years to come, their ilk will be parodied in Dilbert cartoons that show cubicle-dwelling technologists who are left bewildered and abused by their commercial colleagues in marketing and management.

Most of the attendees have not been with Nortel long; in fact, they were part of Nortel's recent takeover of the UK firm, STC. STC belonged to a different era, of executive-only dining rooms and requests for new pencils requiring forms to be signed in triplicate. This isn't the agile firm that Nortel needs to adapt to a fast-changing technology and communications landscape. A major mindset shift is required, so Nortel is bringing in the big guns. The biggest guru of the day, Tom Peters, has been brought in to address the assembled mass. Together with Robert Waterman, he had written the leadership best seller, *In Search of Excellence*, and has been invited to present the essence of his latest blockbuster, *Liberation Management*, to the assembled engineers.

In *Liberation Management*, Tom Peters challenged conventional wisdom and claimed that these are "crazy times that require crazy organizations and crazy people capable of dealing with it all". Using case studies from around the world, Peters demonstrated how extraordinary transformations were being brought about, using radical, new organisational structures. A stuffy, old-fashioned collection of UK scientists had never seen anything like it. It was loud, compelling, interactive and amusing. The tall and confident former McKinsey consultant strode the stage with skill and confidence. It was not just the content that he was presenting that was electrifying; it was the panache with which he did so. And, sat near the front, one person was particularly impressed; a PhD in the field of Human-Computer Interaction, he had recently fallen out of love with computers and had just made the move into the company's training department, and so was part of the team that had booked Peters. He was wowed by both the presentational style and also with the message being passed along, as it resonated so strongly with his own observations and feelings about management.

One particular story stood out to him – that of ABB. ABB was the result of a 1988 merger between a Swedish ASEA and the Swiss business, Brown, Boveri and Cie.

A conglomerate of engineering businesses, ABB had acquired assets ranging from electricity metering to pharmaceuticals. For roughly a decade, from the late 1980s through to the late 1990s, the business press was full of stories about ABB. What could account for their amazing success? Most explanations started at the top with ABB's Chief Executive, Percy Barnevik. He was part of a new breed of business leaders – a Scandinavian, who combined European progressive thinking with American commerciality and orientation for action. A 1991 profile by William Taylor in *Harvard Business Review* described Barnevik as "a corporate pioneer", who was building "the new model of competitive enterprise".

Barnevik considered one of the secrets of his success to be his approach to decision-making:

1. To take action and do the right things is obviously the best behaviour.
2. To take action and do the wrong things is the next best.
3. Not to take action is the only unacceptable behaviour.

It wasn't just his decisive action orientation that mattered; it was also the way in which he had constructed his business. To meet both global and local objectives, ABB had devised a matrix structure of seven major sectors, divided into business areas on one axis and dozens of countries on the other axis. As a result, ABBs matrix had 51 business areas and 41 country managers, which intersected in 1,300 separate companies. These companies were divided into 5,000 profit centres, each one accountable to deliver profits, and empowered to achieve high performance. Critically, each centre had only 50-100 people working in it.

In *Liberation Management*, Tom Peters called ABB "a buckyball organisation", referring to the elegant carbon-based structures designed by Buckminster Fuller, and elsewhere called the "Buckminsterfullerene". A buckyball is a complex, molecular sphere made up of 60 carbon atoms, and Peters likened it to the 50-person business units in ABB. This number of people or carbon atoms was supposedly able to arrange themselves in a particularly strong and interconnected manner. The idea of lots of interconnected, but fully empowered business units was captivating. Rather than the crude, old hierarchy of the past, ABB was designed on a human scale. These groups of 50-100 people could really understand what they were trying to achieve, who their customers were, and connect with their colleagues; it was surely a recipe for success. Rather than having leaders as empire builders, trying to lead armies of thousands, wouldn't it make much more sense to have small, agile and highly motivated groups of people?

Even the guru-sceptics, John Micklethwait and Adrian Wooldridge, who wrote the critically-titled *The Witch Doctors*, set aside their scepticism when it came to ABB. They declared, "Europe has worryingly few management superstars, but one man who unquestioningly fits the bill is Percy Barnevik, a tall, fast-talking Swede with a restless manner of a man over-endowed with energy. Barnevik has won almost every honour which his profession can bestow from emerging markets, CEO of the year to boss of Europe's most respected company." Other books were equally keen to give praise – *ABB: The Dancing Giant* by Kevin Barham and Claudia Heimer being perhaps the most comprehensive.

At the end of the presentation, our "hero", who you by now have certainly guessed is me, was first in the queue for a signed copy of the great book. I still have it now, sat on a bookshelf in my home. Not for the last time in my career, I was a convert, an advocate and a champion for the thinking of a guru. In my youthful enthusiasm, I even tried to pen my own build on the great man's work. I called it *The Chaotic Catalyst* and took this wonderful buckyball idea to a logical conclusion of a world where nobody ever had to work in a business unit of more than 50-100 people. Luckily, nobody was interested in publishing it, because just as I was building my enthusiasm for ABB and Tom Peters' view of it, things were beginning to unravel.

In June 1997, after more than a dozen years at the helm of ABB, Percy Barnevik turned over responsibilities as Chief Executive to Göran Lindahl, and in 1999, Lindahl was named CEO of the Year by *Industry Week*, becoming the first European to receive the award and joining previous winners such as Jack Welch, Michael Deli and Bill Gates. It seems that the glory of ABB wasn't just down to one man, maybe it was the buckyball structure itself, which was great (although Barnevik was still around as Chairman).

However, in April 2001, ABB reported a 6% decline. Combustion Engineering, a US firm it had acquired in 1989, was a target of asbestos litigation, which forced ABB to set aside $470 million as provisions. By autumn 2001, ABB's share price had fallen by 70%. Barnevik resigned as ABB's non-executive Chairman in November

2001, and in 2002, the world learned that Barnevik, and even Lindahl, had secured a secret pension worth $150m. Under intense pressure, Barnevik agreed to return much of it, but their reputations were damaged.

When times were good, ABB's culture had been celebrated by everyone, including me, as bold and daring. Action had been preferred to lengthy analysis and small business units were empowered to turn on a dime and respond to opportunity. But as problems arose, something interesting happened. ABB's ambitious growth strategies were perceived differently and were instead described as impulsive and foolish.

As long as times were good, the complex matrix organisation had been described as a key to its success – buckyballs were the ultimate way for a global firm to be responsive to fast-changing, local needs. Now, a different story started to be told. ABB's poor performance was now attributed to that very same structure. According to The Wall Street Journal, "the decentralised management structure that Mr Barnevik created for the company's far-flung units ended up causing conflicts and communication problems between departments".

The interesting thing was that nobody was suggesting that ABB had abandoned its innovative leadership approach and organisational design. It wasn't thought that they had started to ignore their own recipe for success; instead, that success formula, that panacea for the ills of big business, was now seen more as poison than medicine.

When times were good, Barnevik had been the focus of a virtual personality cult; I looked up to him and admired him myself as a charismatic, bold and visionary leader. But once ABB began to perform poorly, the whole narrative changed. Barnevik was then described as arrogant and resistant to criticism. The two key things that together seemed to make for success – decisive leadership and empowered organisational structures – were now described as a killer combination of arrogance and chaos.

I would love to say that I learned an early lesson about the pitfalls of buying into neatly-packaged solutions, but that would be a lie. Time and again, I have met leadership thinkers, CEOs and politicians who have impressed me with their clarity of vision and have spurred me to action. Time and again, disaster has struck and I have asked myself, "Why didn't I see that coming?" So I offer up this other provisional title for the book: *Why Have I Been A Mug All My Life?*

Of course, I am not alone; many people have been influenced by the big thinkers of our time. We have absorbed, believed and acted on their advice, impressed by their depth of research and clarity of vision. The modern gurus are almost without exception experienced, super-intelligent, credible and compelling. No wonder they have always influenced us. So instead of writing a book about our gullibility, I have sought to understand why it is that, for all their talents, these gurus fail to give us the panacea that we crave. Of course, the quick and simple answer is that there is no panacea, so that is why any attempt to provide one is doomed, but I would like to go a little deeper. Why is it not possible to find a panacea? Why is it so easy for us to convince ourselves that we have found one? I do not believe that the gurus of our world are fools and charlatans, far from it. In the main, I believe that they are highly intelligent people with the positive intent to figure the world out and, in so doing, make it a better place. This book is not an attack on these thinkers, but it does seek to understand why it is so easy for them to get things wrong, and why it is so easy for us to believe them. Furthermore, I will explore what lessons can be learned from them. While things may not be as simple and predictable as they claim, surely there are some insights that they have that can be adopted to increase the likelihood of your business succeeding and your leadership attracting followers. This book aims to help you find these insights and apply them in your own life.

In the decades that followed the Tom Peters presentation, I became a business psychologist and leadership specialist, eventually getting to be the Co-CEO of YSC – one of the world's leading firms in this area. I have therefore been in a world surrounded with leadership gurus, and have had the pleasure of meeting some of the biggest, and occasionally most notorious, CEOs in the world. As such, most of the examples that I will talk about in this book come from the world of leadership and business. However, the reasons for their failings apply to a range of other disciplines, from economics to sport, from health and diet to politics; the insights that gurus give us so often turn out to be wrong. I hope that by explaining the underlying reasons why mistakes are so prevalent, you, the reader, will be better equipped to evaluate the next person who tells you that they have figured it all out.

The Prevalence Of Guru Failure Is Revealed

Rather than waiting around to find the next big guru, I actually went back to earlier management theories. In the period between my reading of *Liberation Management* and the collapse of ABB, I read Peter's original bestseller that he had written with Robert Waterman back in 1982. In a similar formula to his later work, Peters and Waterman had identified 43 of the most amazing companies in the world, and then sought to understand the secret of their success. They wrote their findings up in *In Search of Excellence*, which neatly summarised their discovery of eight practices that are consistently shown by the best companies. These practices were:

1. **A bias for action** – a preference for doing something – anything – rather than sending a question through cycles and cycles of analysis and committee reports.
2. **Staying close to the customer** – learning customer preferences and catering to them.
3. **Autonomy and entrepreneurship** – breaking the corporation into small companies and encouraging them to think independently and competitively.
4. **Productivity through people** – creating in all employees the awareness that their best efforts are essential and that they will share in the rewards of the company's success.
5. **Hands-on, value-driven** – insisting that executives keep in touch with the firm's essential business.

6. **Stick to the knitting** – remaining with the business that the company knows best.
7. **Simple form, lean staff** – few administrative layers, few people at the upper levels.
8. **Simultaneous loose-tight properties** – autonomy within business units, but centralised values.

You know what? Even after more than 30 years, these sound to me like a very sensible set of practices. I don't disagree with them and they seem to work. Even now, I believe that successful companies will almost always be described in terms of these and similar characteristics. Case closed? Well, by now, you must be figuring out that things are not quite that simple.

In 1984, *Business Week* ran a story under the title, *Oops! Who is Excellent Now?* According to this account, at least 14 of the companies highlighted by Peters and Waterman just two years earlier had already started to show the cracks. They went on to explain that these 14 had "suffered significant earnings decline that stem from serious business problems, management problems, or both."

To find out how well the "excellent" companies fared, business professor, Phil Rosenzweig (2007), looked to Compustat®, a leading business database run by Standard and Poor's, and calculated the total shareholder return (that is the per cent change in stock price with all dividends reinvested) for 35 of the "excellent" companies. For various reasons, not all of the 43 could be tracked. He found that "between 1980 and 1984, while the S&P 500 almost doubled, growing by 99%, only 12 "excellent" companies grew faster than the overall market. The other 23 failed to keep up."

Michelle Clayman (1987) conducted a similar study. She retrospectively picked a portfolio of companies with the opposite financial credentials to those selected by Peters and Waterman and found these "anti-excellent" companies performed 60% better than the "excellent" ones over a five-year period.

Let's stop and think about this for the moment. Peters and Waterman had gone out and found what, by all accounts, were really excellent companies. They had found them by asking partners in McKinsey who the really great and interesting companies were. They originally found 62, but boiled this down to 43 by studying the business performance of these businesses and then choosing the best. Yet, these businesses, carefully selected by the best minds in the field, were in subsequent years less likely to perform than the general market. What was going on? Were the eight perfectly sensible business practices that each of these companies seemed to show somehow flawed? Maybe there was something wrong with the Peters approach? Maybe I needed another guru.

Other Gurus Who Have Got It Wrong

Having been let down by one guru, I wasn't put off. The next shining stars to show me the way came in the forms of James Collins and Jerry Porras in their stunning 1994 bestseller, *Built to Last: Successful Habits of Visionary Companies*.

Collins and Porras identified 18 "best of the best" companies, which they then christened "visionary". For each of these so-called "visionary" companies, they also identified "comparison" companies from the same industry, of about the same age, and that were actually pretty good performers. For example, Citicorp had Chase Manhattan as a comparator and Hewlett-Packard had Texas Instruments. By comparing the "visionary" with the "comparison companies", they didn't just want to see "good" management practice; they really wanted to see what it was that set apart the superstars.

As seems to be the practice of leadership gurus, they came up with a list of attributes that, if followed, I presumed would allow me to lead my growing list of corporate clients on the path to greatness. Here is their list:

1. Having a strong, core ideology that guides the company's decisions and behaviour.
2. Building a strong, corporate culture.
3. Setting audacious goals that can inspire and stretch people.
4. Developing people and promoting from within.
5. Creating a spirit of experimentation and risk-taking.
6. Driving for excellence.

Again, this seems to me to be a pretty good list, and not a million miles away from the Peters and Waterman conclusions.

So how did the "visionary" companies fare by following this particular formula? Once again, Rosenzweig looked at it. He found that, in 2000, 18 were still up and running (so at least they were built to last for 10 years), but the performance wasn't stunning. He looked at total shareholder return of the visionary companies from 1991 to 1995. Remember, these were companies that were chosen because they had a history of outperforming the market in a huge way, so you might expect them to continue to do well. In reality, he found that only eight of them did better than the S&P average, while the others lagged behind. He concluded:

> "You would have been better off investing randomly than putting your money on Collins and Porras' Visionary companies."

Interestingly, he also tried to track the "comparison" companies and, of the twelve that could be tracked, seven beat the S&P and only five did worse. Once again, my world was rocked, but not in a good way. If Rosenzweig's analysis was to be believed, I might have been giving my clients entirely the wrong advice. I was telling them to emulate the "visionary", but maybe they would have been better of copying the "comparison" group. It just didn't make sense. Look back at the six attributes of "visionary" companies. They are pretty good, aren't they? What can be wrong with "Driving for Excellence"? Should we all instead pursue mediocrity? Obviously not. It seems to me that, like Peters, they had come up with a pretty good list. The problem seems to be that following this list is no guarantee of future success. It is not the magic cure-all. It is not the panacea. Those that we were being encouraged to emulate appeared to be faring no better than anyone else.

*   *   *

In true Tom Peters' style, Collins left his co-author and went it alone in 2001 with *Good to Great: Why Some Companies Make the Leap... and Others Don't*. Collins looked at companies that had 15 years of stock market returns near the general average, which was then punctuated by a transition point, followed by 15 years of stock market returns well above the average, giving a "hockey stick" shaped growth curve. A single dollar invested in this group of companies in 1965 with all dividends reinvested would have grown to $471 by the end of 2000, compared to $56 from the overall market. Once again, he also identified a group of "comparison" companies to match each of the "great" ones. A dollar invested in the "comparison" companies in 1965 would have only grown to $93, still better than the market but nowhere near the "great".

Managers of these companies were asked to look back and explain what had happened as nobody had had the foresight to capture the realities at the time. The questioning identified a number of phases to the growth of the "great" companies. The **Build-up Phase** comes first, and is characterised by strong, yet humble leadership (known as Level Five Leadership), getting people on board and facing reality directly and courageously. It is then followed by a point of inflection, leading to the **Breakthrough Phase** of great growth and success. The inflection point is when the company figures out what is really going to make the difference, then commits to it wholeheartedly. The book seems to suggest that the "great" companies were focussed on a unifying vision, rather than having their attention scattered. Unlike previous books, this one wasn't trying to predict which of these companies were following a formula that would predict future success; rather it was trying to identify those who had done something well in the past, and so criticising what came next for any of these companies would not be fair.

However, we can still detect a flaw that might make us pause before following their example. One of the reasons for these companies succeeding was that they had thought hard then bet big on a defining strategy, rather than scattering their attention and hedging their bets. When big betters win, they win big. On average, they massively outperform those lily-livered souls who want to try to be all things to all men. But not all bets pay off. We don't even get to hear of the thousands who fail. Should we follow the example of those highly-focussed success stories? It isn't really clear, as Collins hadn't studied the companies who had behaved in the same way and failed.

It seems that the Guru Failure tendency isn't a quirk of Tom Peters. The greatest names in leadership literature are all prone to it. The apparently simple task of finding successful businesses and trying to distil what makes them successful appears to be fundamentally flawed. We really need to understand why it is so hard to learn lessons from companies that are doing well, companies like Cisco.

The Cisco Story

One of the more extraordinary business stories of recent years is Cisco. In their book, *Hidden Value: How Great Companies Achieve Extraordinary Results with Ordinary People*, Charles O'Reilly III and Jeffrey Pfeffer refer to Cisco's management of acquisitions and noted its ability to retain talent.

> "Think about it deductively, Cisco was more successful than other companies so that must mean it has been more adept than its competitors at providing customers with technology and equipment they want. And that meant two things; Cisco has a strong belief in having no technology religion, and listening carefully to customers."

That was what Cisco really did well – it listened intently to customers. It watched where the market was going, then acquired the necessary technology and retained the people who developed it. The key to Cisco's success has everything to do its ability to tap into the talent and energy of its workforce.

Sounds great, doesn't it? It also happens to match my own beliefs about business success, a focus on both customers and talent. Indeed, as I make my living in the world of talent management, I couldn't have been happier about their conclusions. However, by the end of 2000, Cisco's share price had dropped all the way to $38, which was less than half of its record high.

Fortune 2001 contained an article titled *Cisco Fractures Its Own Fairy Tale*.

"On the way to a stock market value of half a trillion dollars, everything about Cisco seemed perfect. It had a perfect CEO. It could close its books in a day and make perfect financial forecasts. It was an acquisition machine, ingesting companies and technologies with great aplomb. It was the leader of the new economy, selling gear to new-world telecom companies that would use it to supplant old-world carriers and make their old-world suppliers irrelevant. Over the past year, every one of those characterizations has proved to be false."

What about its extreme customer focus? Now *Fortune 2001* reported that Cisco "had exhibited a cavalier attitude towards potential customers". Cisco's sales techniques had been "irksome" and had "alienated" customers. Cisco had been "basking in a culture of confidence" that its venture into telecom products was evidence of Cisco's "swagger", and that its "assuredness bordered on the naïve".

Of course, the Cisco story doesn't end there; they turned themselves around and more greatness was to come. Did they rediscover their mojo? Had they ever lost it in the first place? Did they abandon their customer focus and slip as a result, only to recover it later? We desperately struggle to make sense of the story, to explain success and failure in the hope that we can replicate the former and avoid the latter. Maybe it is that very search for narrative that is the problem; an issue that I will explore in detail in Chapter 1.

Some More Examples Of Guru Let-Downs

Of course, I am not the first to spot the frequent errors of gurus; some of the greatest names of our time have drawn attention to it. Take this quote from Matthew Stewart's (2009) book, *The Management Myth*:

> "In their 1994 book, *Competing for the Future*, Hamel and Prahalad spill the ink for, among others, General Magic, a venture that aspired to unite the world with intelligent personal communication devices. General Magic vanished like pixie dust with the emergence of the Internet and cell phones. '[Hamel and Prahalad] are probably as good as there is in their field,' Bill Gates commented in 1998. But 'every example they gave, with the exception of Hewlett Packard, was a total joke'. By the time Gates had made this comment, however, Hamel had moved on, now touting Enron as America's 'most innovative company'"

This seems as good a time as any to touch on that Enron story. We are all familiar with its failure – the large-scale accounting fraud that led to its bankruptcy in 2001 and bringing down its accountancy firm, Arthur Andersen, at the same time. What we sometimes forget is how Enron had been perceived before it all went wrong. While some *Fortune* magazine journalists helped unearth the issues, that same publication named it America's Most Innovative Company every year from 1996 to 2001, and in 2000, had it on the list of the 100 Best Companies to Work for in America.

According to Rosenzweig:

> "Enron had actually been a poster child for innovation in Gary Hamel's (later revised) book, *Leading the Revolution*. At Harvard Business School, case studies have been written about Enron's creativity and innovative business model, only to disappear from the HBS catalogue in the wake of Enron's collapse, where they were replaced with cautionary case studies about corruption and leadership gone astray."

That's right; when they were doing well, Enron were looked to as a role model. Not because we were foolish, but because they were clearly doing well and everyone wanted a sip of the magic potion that they appeared to have. In the late 90s, learned and sensible commentators would have encouraged you to model your business after Enron, and they would have had a string of valid reasons for doing so. When we look to follow the example of success, do we really know what we are doing? Time and again, we latch onto the apparently successful and believe that we can be like them. Can we really? Should we really? These are the questions that will be explored in this book.

Where Else Do Gurus Get It Wrong?

It may be that I am unlucky enough to work in a field that has a monopoly on gurus who make mistakes, but I doubt it. It seems to me that, across a wide range of walks of life, similar things are happening. Take politics, for example, in the UK, one time Chancellor of the Exchequer, Gordon Brown, declared, "Under this Government, Britain will not return to the boom and bust of the past." A decade earlier, Margaret Thatcher's army of new homeowners promised a similar economic miracle. Neither political doctrine got it right.

Similarly, the world of finance has no end of people selling their expertise at predicting which shares will rise in value and which will fall, but on close examination, their claims lack substance. In Burton G. Malkiel's frequently republished classic, *Random Walk Down Wall Street*, he boldly declares "... a blindfolded chimpanzee throwing darts at the stock listings can select a portfolio that performs as well as those managed by the experts."

The False Panacea That Was Black-Scholes

Gordon Brown's apparent belief that he had found a magic formula is hardly unique in the world of economics. Take, for example, the Black-Scholes formula for pricing derivatives. This even won its creator a Nobel Prize in 1997. By applying this formula, investors would no longer be dependent on luck or feel for the market. Indeed, if the world continued to behave the way that it always had, it was apparently a way to make money without the risk of ever losing it. Science had discovered a way of taking the chance out of investment. Having made such a discovery, Scholes wasn't afraid to put his money where his mouth was and so founded the hedge fund, Long-Term Capital Management (LTCM). At first, things seemed to be working with three years of profit in excess of 20%.

The problem came when the real-world environment stopped matching the formulas that they had put into their model. There was an unexpected Russian default that came hot on the heels of the Asian financial crisis. These large-scale events effectively broke the model. This is how Ed Smith describes what happened next:

> "LTCM's models told them they shouldn't expect to lose more than $50 million on any given day, ever. But four days after Russia defaulted, they dropped half a billion dollars in one day. The concept of finance without chance or uncertainty had gone spectacularly bust."

Self-Help Gurus And Success Stories Outside Of Business

The most common realm for the guru to inhabit is not leadership but self-help. Not only do we look to the many writers and motivational speakers in this area, we also absorb the many memoirs and autobiographies of successful people who kindly share the secrets of their success. Many of the gurus in this place will also follow a similar "research" pattern to those leadership gurus discussed in this chapter. In essence, they look at groups of very rich and successful people and try to figure out what they have in common (apart from the fame and money). The output of these works includes incredibly successful guides such Stephen Covey's *Seven Habits of Highly Successful People*.

Clearly, every story and every guru is unique, but some common themes emerge. Without meaning to simplify an entire industry, I think I can summarise a lot of success insight into four principles:

1. Believe in yourself.
2. Visualise the success you seek.
3. Practise.
4. Persevere.

These often-repeated principles seem to have a lot going for them. It is easy to see how they can be of help. Indeed, it is easy for those who have succeeded to reflect on their lives and recognise these attributes. It is also easy to imagine how disabling it must be to be a self-doubter who gives up at the first sign of challenge. To most people, I would be described as highly successful in my career and private life. I am confident in my abilities, have shown resilience in the face of obstacles, and I have even used the techniques in Point 2 above. I have set my goals and imagined myself achieving them, and I have certainly put in the required 10,000 hours of practice. I am perhaps a living example that these self-help gurus have got it right. And yet... my experiences as a leadership professional and repeated guru-sucker have led me to doubt the truth of these four beliefs.

If the self-help industry has really found the secret of success, then that implies that those whose lives have not been as charmed as mine must have somehow failed to follow the good advice, and this just does not ring true. The world that I have experienced (from Lagos to Mumbai, from Dhaka to Mexico City) is full of people who have hearts of lions, dream every day of a brighter future and never give up, but they aren't all celebrities or billionaires; most of them are struggling to survive from one day to the next. People who follow the self-help rules sit at every strata of society and are in every country around the world. They comprise winners and losers, success and failure, the rich and the poor, the healthy and the ill.

At best, these books help people to make their lives a little better, but at worst, they leave people feeling to blame for their own misfortunes. They may be left feeling that if their dreams do not come true, it must be due to their own lack of self-belief or for not persevering enough. Indeed, the implied criticism can be even worse than that. Consider the following quote from the bestselling author of *The Secret*, Rhonda Byrne:

"In a large-scale tragedy, like 9/11, Hurricane Katrina, etc., we see that the law of attraction responds to people being at the wrong place at the wrong time because their dominant thoughts were on the same frequency of such events... If their dominant thoughts and feelings were in alignment with the energy or fear, separation, powerlessness and having no control over outside circumstances, then that is what they attracted.

"Remember, while many people died in these tragic events, there were also many miraculous stories of survival. And the same can be said about those people whose thoughts were in alignment with the energy of unity, love, oneness and joy with the universe."

As Ed Smith rightly observes, "This comes dangerously close to implying that it's your fault if you find yourself in the middle of a hurricane, or, indeed, a holocaust."

Sport And Fitness

Sporting professionals have taken some of the themes mentioned above to an extreme degree, and in doing so, have demonstrated a great paradox of gurus – the ability to be both right and wrong at the same time. Sport psychologists now play a vital role in the coaching and support of professional athletes. Many of their techniques share the philosophes of the self-help gurus. In particular, they make use of the power of visualisation. Whether it be picturing the perfect putt in golf or visualising victory in a tennis match, sporting stars will frequently attribute their success to their absolute belief in their own ability to succeed and the certainty that picturing themselves on the podium has given them. I do not believe that such approaches would not be so widely used if they did not provide some benefit. In fact, it is hard to find someone who doesn't use them, and that is where the paradox arises. Every time that a top professional goes out on the field of play picturing their own certainty of success, they are faced with an opponent who has done exactly the same thing. At most, only one of them can be right. So are the gurus wrong in teaching the importance of visualising success? No, I don't think so. But, by simple logic, the techniques that they teach lead to failure as frequently as they lead to success. Perhaps when our business leaders attribute their success to customer focus, or keeping things simple, they are not wrong in thinking that those things helped, but they may be wrong in thinking that they explained their success on their own, as their less-successful competitors probably did the same thing too.

The Red Pill

This book takes its title from a recurrent motif in science fiction – the red pill. While it has appeared in a range of settings, most people remember it from the movie, *The Matrix*. On discovering that the world he lives in may not be as real as he thought, the hero is offered the choice of pills. A blue pill will allow him to return to the comfy illusion that he has been living in the past. The red pill will reveal the truth, but it is clear that the truth may be a lot harder to handle than the illusion.

So consider this book your own red pill. You can put it down and return to the usual management books that provide simple answers and reassuring stories. Alternatively, you can take the red pill and read on. I will certainly take you down a lot of rabbit holes, and the truth will not offer an easy panacea, but you will discover a way to be the leader you wish to be, even after you have seen things as they really are.

References

Barham, Kevin (1998) *ABB The Dancing Giant: Creating the Globally Connected Company*

Business Week (1984) *Oops! Who is Excellent Now*? (November 5) pp.76-88

Clayman, Michelle (May-June, 1987) *In Search of Excellence: The Investor's Viewpoint. Financial Analysts Journal.* pp.54-63.

Collins, James (2005) *Built to Last: Successful Habits of Visionary Companies*

Collins, Jim (2001) *Good to Great*

Hamel, Gary (2002) *Leading the Revolution: How to Thrive in Turbulent Times by Making Innovation a Way of Life*

Malkiel, Burton G. (2012) *A Random Walk Down Wall Street: The Time-Tested Strategy for Successful Investing (Ninth Edition)*

Mehta, Stephanie (May 2001) *Cisco Fractures Its Own Fairy Tale, Fortune*

Micklethwait, John and Wooldridge, Adrian (1997) *The Witch Doctors: What the Management Gurus are Saying, Why it Matters and How to Make Sense of it*

O'Reilly, Charles and Pfeffer, Jeffrey (2000) *Hidden Value: How Great Companies Achieve Extraordinary Results with Ordinary People*

Peters, Tom (1992) *Liberation Management: Necessary Disorganization for the Nanosecond Nineties*

Peters, Tom and Waterman Jr, Robert (1982*) In Search of Excellence: Lessons from America's Best-Run Companies*

Rosenzweig, Phil (2007) *The Halo Effect... and Eight Other Business Delusions That Deceive Managers*

Smith, Ed (2012) *Luck: A Fresh Look at Fortune*

Syed, Matthew (2010) *Bounce: The Myth of Talent and the Power of Practice*

Taylor, William (March/April, 1991) *"The logic of Global Business: An Interview with ABB's Percy Barnevik", Harvard Business Review*

Overview of This Book

Over the following chapters, I will introduce you to a range of reasons why business writers of all types fail to live up to our expectations and why our longed-for panaceas turn out to be less effective that we hope. This book unearths the wide range of reasons why conventional writers get it wrong and then, having revealed the truth, explores how you can still extract value from their work, despite the problems and errors.

Chapter 1 – *Customers First: Why only the good stories get told* examines the sources of the stories we get to hear. They tend to be written by consultants, journalists and academics; people who are on the outside of organisations rather than the inside. As a result, they only get access and permission to tell positive stories and they only get the truth of failure after the fact. I will explore why our desire for everything to be packaged into a neat story is in itself an unrealistic desire that inevitably leads to distortion and over-simplification. I will reveal how to use stories without being blinded by them.

Chapter 2 – *Playing Chicken with a Cliff: Why past success doesn't always predict future success* takes a look at one of our fundamental beliefs that, time and again, leads us into trouble – the implicit belief that the past predicts the future. Surely, we think, the stock-picker who outperformed the market last year is the best person to follow when investing next year. It seems reasonable, but is it actually true? If not, why not? And what can we do if the future is so inherently unpredictable.

Chapter 3 – *The Smartest Guys in the Room: The compelling nature of CEOs* introduces you to some of the most amazing and successful people in the world – CEOs, politicians and academics. In their chosen fields or businesses, they are hard, if not impossible, to argue with. But if they are all so convincing, how are you and I to know which ones to believe in and which ones to ignore? I will show you how to learn from these big characters without falling into the trap of joining a personality cult.

Chapter 4 – *It's Just Maths: How statistics can explain why good companies get worse* takes a close look at this mathematics, as many of the great arguments that business writers make are based on numbers, facts and data. By demystifying the numbers, you can begin to see through the claims, theories and hypotheses, and understand why it is so hard to predict both success and failure in any walk of life. You can also learn what facts are mathematically true and which are false.

Chapter 5 – *Dedicated Followers of Fashion: Why we all want the latest, big thing* explores the fickle nature of fads. It looks at whether our insatiable need to be ahead of others in understanding the next big thing creates a market for fresh insights, which causes us to see them where they do not really exist. You will learn to uncover the enduring truths of leadership and not just the latest spin.

Chapter 6 – *Living in a Bubble: Why gurus are always part of the illusion of the day* introduces us to the almost intractable problem that we are all part of the phenomenon that we are trying to observe and understand. Is it ever possible to stand far enough away from the world in which we live to gain an accurate perspective on it? By broadening our perspective, a whole new way to live as a leader will emerge.

Chapter 7 – *Too Much of a Good Thing: How all strengths can be overdone* delves into one of the practical issues that arises when improving anything, be it yourself, your business, society or anything else. Strengths, positive behaviours and secrets of success can all be over-done. That which is most admired can be your undoing, so pointing to the characteristics of success is often the same thing as pointing to the seeds of your own destruction. You will learn how to maximise your strengths without letting them become your undoing.

Chapter 8 – *Hall of Mirrors: The impact of observation on the observed* looks at the impact of being in the limelight. You will see how, time and again, companies and people have been altered by the positive press they have received; the trouble that starts when they start to believe the story being told. I will explore how to avoid hubris and the corruption of power that so often accompanies success. We will learn to maximise the benefit of feedback to steer us on the right course.

Chapter 9 – *Show Me the Money: Solutions sell* looks at the financial imperative behind the work of business consultants of every type. Unless a solution can be found, there is nothing to sell. Even in writing this book, the first question I was asked was, "So what is your solution? Who is getting it right?" This pressure for an answer always provides an answer; the problem is that it is not necessarily the right one. By understanding the economic driver of the writers you read, you can really learn to separate the insight from the spin.

Chapter 10 – *No More Heroes Any More: The red pill leader is revealed* continues that search for the elusive hero – that someone who has got it right, is still getting it right, and will continue to get it right in the future. I will give my own thoughts on what we can learn from the many stories contained in this book and how we should therefore seek to live our lives, be we the leaders or the led.

Throughout this book, you will learn much about the failure of management gurus to deliver that elusive panacea, but this does not render all their advice useless. If we can understand the reasons why they get things wrong and unearth the many ways in which we delude ourselves, I don't believe that we are left with a pile of broken promises. Instead, we can begin to take the lessons and stories for what they are and we can find the whispers of wisdom that help us find our own paths as leaders or people. Having taken the red pill, you will be in a position to move beyond being a follower of others and instead, become your own guru.

Chapter 1

Customers First:
Why Only The Good
Stories Get Told

"To hell with facts! We need stories!"
Ken Kesey

For many years, the Co-operative Bank seemed to be somewhat of an ethical beacon in the world of banking. With its origins in the co-operative movement, I associated them with fairness, decency, and being on the side of the ordinary person. Their place in UK society made the crisis that they faced in 2013 big news. A rescue plan was needed following the revelation that they had a £1.9 billion capital shortfall. In the aftermath, Sir Christopher Kelly was asked to conduct an independent review of what went wrong. His thorough 151-page report summarises the reasons for the failing as follows:

1. The economic environment (particularly low interest rates) that lasted for a sustained period.
2. The regulator requirements for capital were continually increased following the global financial crisis.

3. The merger with another lender who had higher than expected impairments on their books.
4. Failure to plan capital adequately, post-merger.
5. Poor risk management.
6. Lack of adequate experience in a number of senior positions.
7. In common with most other banks, Payment Protection Insurance (PPI) was considered to be miss-sold and so funding was needed for compensation claims.
8. A number of cultural weaknesses, such as an unwillingness to challenge people.
9. The poor governance flowing from the way in which board members were elected.

This very long and thorough review shows how many issues can combine to bring a bank to the edge of ruin. However, this full analysis doesn't make for a very engaging story, does it? I don't think that I had you excited and engaged by my retelling of these highlights. Believe me; the full report would have gripped you even less. Perhaps then, it is no surprise that if you ask anyone in the UK why Co-op Bank hit trouble, they will have a much more juicy story to tell – the story that gave us headlines like this.

Rev's drugs with rent boys.

Paul Flowers, the Methodist minister with meth in his madness.

Bank ex-chairman on crack and meth after debt disaster.

Paul Flowers, the Methodist minister and former Rochdale councillor embroiled in a drugs and rent boy scandal.

Journalists had caught a drug deal on film involving Paul Flowers, who was Chairman of Co-operative Bank when things were going wrong. In addition to the drugs and prostitution claims, it was also highlighted that he lacked significant banking experience. The story now was much more simple and scandalous to retell. This flawed person must be the person to blame for Co-op's failings. How reassuring for us all to learn that if we can make sure our chairman understands our business and keep off the crack, we are totally safe from disaster – such a neat morality tale for our times.

Despite the clearly negative slant of this tale, the sub-title of this chapter originated from my observation that, in general, only very positive stories ended up being told. There were countless stories of success that were shared so that others might emulate that success. So this chapter will explore the reasons why we mainly see good stories (if you define good as being a tale of success), and what the implication of that bias might be. However, the recent global financial crisis and a stream of scandals like the one above has led to a shift in that balance, and we can now find an abundance of cautionary tales. However, I have chosen to keep the title intact as it seems to me that these are still "good stories" in that they follow a neat narrative pattern. In this chapter, we will see that the attraction we have to neatly-packaged tales turns out to be one of the reasons that business writers so often get things wrong.

"Good Stories" Of Failure

There has always been a market for a story of failure. It can't follow the formula of "I will share the secret of success", which is so clearly bankable, but there is room in the market for cautionary tales. If the guru in question can construct the right narrative around why the company failed, then it is possible to sell a solution that will help you avoid making the same mistake. Maybe it is even better to tell us a success story and failure story at the same time. In *Strategic IQ*, John Wells from Harvard Business School gives us good accounts of the failure of both K-Mart and Circuit City. He combines it with the success of Walmart and Best Buy to teach us the benefit of what he terms "strategic IQ".

Since the Global Financial Crisis, a new type of failure story has become very popular with leadership writers. It is the story of corporate greed, excess, corruption and resultant failure. Whether we are discussing Northern Rock or RBS in the UK, or Enron and Lehman in the US, journalists and academics alike seem to have uncovered very neat morality tales for us to digest. At the heart of these stories is likely to be the evil or misguided CEO – a CEO who once rode high and was admired by all, but has now been dragged down by some character flaw.

In *The Seven Basic Plots: Why we tell stories*, Christopher Booker describes for us the prevalence of these characters in fiction.

> "The essence of the tragic hero or heroine, said Aristotle, is that they must not be shown as wholly good or bad, but that they must be shown as being brought from 'prosperity to

misery' through some 'fatal flaw'. And the Greek work for this was hamartia, which means literally 'missing the mark', as an arrow fails to reach its target. The fatal flaw in the tragic hero or heroine is that deficiency in their character or awareness that prevents them from 'reaching their goal'."

These are the stories of Icarus or Anakin Skywalker in fiction, transferred onto Skilling or Goodwin in the world of business.

We love the idea of the fatal flaw, in part because it can make us feel more secure in a volatile world. We can say to ourselves that they failed because of a flaw, so if I can avoid this flaw, I will be safe. It gives us a sense of agency, that we can master our own destiny. We can also feel superiority or schadenfreude in relation to these people we previously envied. The reality that terrible things can happen to your business, even when you are apparently doing everything right, is too unsettling a thought to bear.

The Bias Towards Sharing Positive News

Let's now go on to my original interpretation of "good", the success stories; why are so many books written about successful companies and all the amazing things those companies did to become successful? The obvious answer would be that this is because success is exactly what people want to read about, but the salacious tale at the start of this chapter shows that there is just a big a market for failure. I therefore believe that there is a much more fundamental reason why so many stories are of success; it is about access, confidentiality clauses and the desire of consultants to keep their valuable clients happy.

As a consultant myself, I have had amazing exposure to the top of big businesses, I have discussed the inner concerns of business leaders and sat around the table while commercial strategy has been set. In the course of doing so, I have seen brilliance and foolishness, which was sometimes apparent at the time and sometimes only with the benefit of hindsight. Now let us suppose that I wish to share those stories so that you might learn from them. Well, unfortunately I can't. You see, in order to be allowed to participate in such conversations, I had to sign confidentiality agreements that prevent me from discussing what I have heard without the prior permission of my client. What kind of story do you think I will ever be given permission to share? There is no way that I am ever going to be able to tell the story of how the CFO's ego got in the way of a sensible compensation plan being agreed, is there? However, I am much more likely to be allowed to tell the story of how the new CEO brought about a more customer-centric culture.

Look again at the work of Peter and Waterman in the Introduction. They came from McKinsey, the leading strategy consultancy, and got their list of "excellent" companies from their fellow consultants. Just how likely was it ever going to be that anything other than an extremely positive narrative was going to emerge?

You might well say that this barrier clearly applies to consultants, but what about the other people who can tell the story – employees, journalists or academics. In general, similar restrictions and dynamics apply to them. How free is any employee to tell the truth about their business? They may have gagging clauses that persist even after they have left the business, and even if they didn't, who would want to employ the person that bad-mouthed their old employer? Journalists occasionally can run great stories of failure, but that is normally after the fact when the truth behind a failure has already begun to leak out. If you want the inside story on a currently thriving company, if you want that CEO interview, how easy will it be to do anything other than a puff piece? Read the next CEO interview you see in a business magazine and I think you will find the answer. Academics too need access, and it is foolish to believe that any access can come without certain restrictions.

Burton Malkiel describes how important journalists feel it is to tell a good business story:

> "CNBC's commentators like Maria (the money honey) Bartiromo particularly favoured scheduling interviews with analysts who could say with confidence that some $50 dot-com stock would soon go to $500. There was no need to remind a CNBC anchor that, just as the family dog that bites the baby is likely to have a short tenure, sourpuss sceptics did not encourage high ratings."

He also highlights the bias that comes from analysts having a vested interest in what they are reporting:

> "An analyst from BNP Paribas alleged that he was forced out of his job after a sell recommendation

on Enron. Small wonder most analysts have purged their prose of negative comments that might give offense to current or prospective investment banking clients. In the 1990s, the ratio of buy to sell recommendations climbed to 100 to 1, particularly for brokerage firms with large investment banking businesses."

It seems that a very wide range of sources that inform our opinions on business are distorted by the relationships those sources have with those businesses. We must understand and be mindful of these influences, therefore, when we are looking at the examples of success that are laid before us.

The Halo Effect

Surely though, we can do something to understand what is going on in the companies, without having to go inside yourself and become trapped in confidentiality clauses and the like. In *The Halo Effect*, Rosenzweig explains how such studies sometimes get constructed. One approach is to ask business leaders in general which company they most admire, which company has the best customer service, which company treats its employees the best, or any one of a hundred questions about businesses in the public eye. When you do this kind of research, you will quickly be able to find some great connections. For example, you will likely find that the most commercially successful companies also have the best focus on customers. There you have it, proof that customer centricity is the key to success. Actually, you will also find that the best companies also have the best supply chain, the best marketing, the most respected brand, the most loyal employees, the list goes on. It turns out that what you have actually got is a perception from the outside, which has been shaped by something called The Halo Effect.

The Halo Effect is the commonly-observed tendency of people to extrapolate beyond one positive characteristic of a person to other traits. For example, if you observe someone who is a successful salesman, you are likely to rate them high in a number of other areas, like organisation, drive and charm (even if you have no direct evidence that they really are good at these things). Some of you may do this because you have your own theory of what a good salesman must be like, and apply this to any person good at sales. You think you know something but you don't actually. Others may simply do this because they have in their mind a number of things that are "good", and it is easy to assume that "good" people are "good" at many things. This halo effect is very prevalent and consistent across situations. Even when we know that it exists, it is hard for us to avoid. We also tend to do the reverse, what is sometimes called the "Horns Effect". This describes our tendency to assume a basket of negative attributes about someone, based on one specific negative observation. The failing employee is often perceived to be bad at everything, even when this isn't true.

The dangers of The Halo Effect really come through in the work of leadership gurus when they conduct studies to determine what makes companies great. If you don't have actual access to top companies, one common methodology of studying them is to seek the perceptions of others about them. Take a group of business leaders and ask them to complete a survey about the most admired and least admired businesses in the world. Ask them about their perceptions of these companies: their marketing, their values, their talent, their IT, the list could go on. I can pretty much guarantee that you will find that the most admired companies in the world are also seen to have the best IT, talent or whatever. You might therefore conclude that the secret to success is their focus on talent, IT, organisation or whatever else you have asked about. In reality, all you have done however is demonstrate The Halo Effect. The people you have asked may have little or no knowledge of the inner workings of these companies, but they will answer the questionnaire anyway and attribute lots of positive things to the successful, and lots of negative things to the unsuccessful, regardless of how true this may be.

We like things to be simple, we like the world to hang together in an ordered manner, and so we construct simple stories and models of the world. If something cannot be packaged in this neat way, it deprives us of the sense of narrative that we like to have in our lives, and especially in our business and leadership books. Messiness does not make for a good story, which in turn does not make for a good business book or a good guru.

What on earth can we do about this problem? Well clearly, the knowledge of The Halo Effect itself at least tells us to be aware of these spurious correlations, but I think it should also cause us to challenge our own perceptions. When we look around us, do we look for too simplistic a divide between good and bad?

Should we rather push ourselves to challenge whether everything the successful leader does is good or whether the struggling business is all bad? Taking the richer and more complex view of life definitely requires more mental effort, so perhaps that is the reason that we opt for simplicity, but think how much more could be achieved by challenging the poor actions of those who are winning and finding merit in the efforts of those who are on the ropes.

The Human Need For Narrative

Deep within all of us, there appears to be a need to make sense of the world in the form of commonly recurring stories. In *The Seven Basic Plots*, Christopher Booker comprehensively analyses centuries of literature to demonstrate the reoccurrence of certain stories. He describes one particular story, which occurred in the most important book of my childhood. I read this book so often that it fell apart and I had to buy a replacement, twice! Here is Booker's description:

> "Once upon a time, there was a young hero or heroine, not yet embarked on adult life, living in lowly or difficult circumstance. This humble little figure, almost certainly an orphan, was regarded as of little worth by most people around, and may even have been actively maltreated. But one day something happened to send our hero or heroine out into the world where they met with a series of adventures that eventually brought about a miraculous transformation of

their fortunes. Emerging from the shadows of their wretched former state, they were raised to a position of dazzling splendour, winning them the admiration of all who beheld them."

Do you recognise it? It was probably your favourite too. It is of course *Aladdin/Cinderella/Dick Whittington/ Eliza Doolittle/David Copperfield/Jane Eyre/The Ugly Duckling* and more. Actually, for me, it was none of these; it was actually a character called Pug in a fantasy novel called *Magician* by Raymond E. Feist. For my children, it is either Harry Potter or Luke Skywalker. They are all variations of the rags to riches story, the most prevalent tale in the world it seems. According to Booker, "Well over 1,000 versions have been collected of the *Cinderella* story alone."

We seem to gravitate towards certain story formulas and this is just one of the seven he explores. In trying to understand what is behind these common themes, Booker notes: "... this tradition has in many ways been built on the perception of Bastian, over a century ago, that the human imagination seems to be constituted that it naturally works around certain 'elemental' shapes and images." Where these elements come from probably varies widely – is it the changing of the seasons, the rising and setting of the sun, birth and death, puberty? Clearly, there are some experiences that we always relate to and stories help us explore them.

So what does this have to do with leadership gurus? Well they too are often storytellers and, as such, they are likely to gravitate to the same basic story plots, even if they are not aware that they are doing so. For example, as Booker says: "... it is likely that a story will have a hero, or a heroine, or both: a central figure, or figures, on whose fate our interests in the story ultimately rests; someone with whom, as we say, we can identify."

So gurus will always be drawn to identifying a hero of the story (usually a CEO) that we can relate to. As a consequence, the importance of that character may be magnified and other important variables may be ignored because they do not contribute to the plotline. Even random things can be attributed to a character in a story.

In *Fooled by Randomness*, Nassim Taleb recalls Bloomberg's coverage of Saddam Hussein's capture in 2003. At first, *Bloomberg News* put up the headline "US treasury bonds rise, Hussein capture may not curb terrorism". Half an hour later, as US treasury bonds fell in price, Bloomberg ran the headline "US treasuries fall; Hussein capture boosts allure of risky assets". The same cause was being used to explain to polar-opposite effects.

We like people to make sense of the world for us. The best way of doing that is to put the events into a familiar story format. Unfortunately, what we end up with is not a scientific analysis of what has actually happened; it is of course a story. An old and familiar story probably, but retold for us again.

How Different Time Horizons Frame The Story

The reality of most organisational stories is complex and variable. Many things impact success, both within and beyond any particular business, and the path of events isn't straight, but has twists turns, ups and downs. A graphical representation of a real organisational story may look something like this. Different lines represent different variables, actors or initiatives.

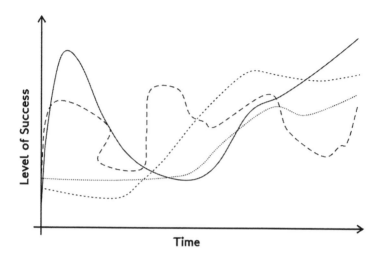

It is confusing and lacks coherence, so the first thing the good storyteller does is thin out the cast of characters.

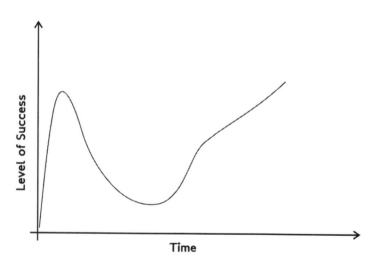

The next thing they do is pick the time horizon that fits the story we want to tell. We could pick the first half of the chart and describe sudden success that led to sudden failure, or the second half of the chart and describe a straightforward success story. These stories may seem valid when presented in isolation, but we must remember that they have been chosen because they are an easy story to tell, not because they represent the whole story. Who wants to hear a story that describes a company that was good at some things and was bad at others, and for whom some years were better than others; overall, it did OK, but it is hard to put your finger on exactly why as these things are complex? Nobody. Yet, unfortunately, that is the reality of most businesses, **even the ones in the guru books**. They have just had a neat version of their story told in order to make a point.

Even Randomness Can Be Spun Into A Story

If it is not bad enough that complex systems are oversimplified into neat stories, it seems that we can apparently create stories for ourselves out of nothing at all, so intense is our desire to see patterns and flow. In *A Random Walk Down Wall Street*, Malkiel devotes time to the discussion of "chartists". These people analyse the ups and downs of stock price performance to try to discern patterns that will help them predict what will happen next. To challenge their approach, Malkiel ran an experiment with his students where, instead of following real stock trades, they determined whether a fictitious stock would rise or fall by the flip of a coin. In doing so, they produced charts that looked a little like this.

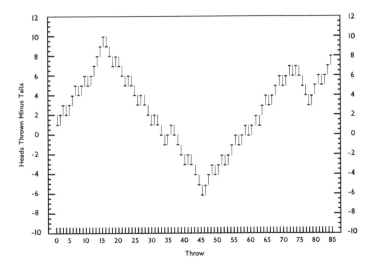

Instead of charts that appear to the human eye to be completely random, it was possible for the coin tosses to give an appearance of patterns and flows. It looks as though sometimes the coin tossing is on an upwards trend and sometimes it is trending downwards. Now we know that, in actual fact, the coin tosses are random, so we would not really believe that there was some underlying trend. By contrast, it is possible that stock market variations are equally random, but when that randomness creates smooth flows, as in the chart above, we can falsely attribute an upwards curve to a stock being on a positive run for some good business reason. In reality, it is just our human tendency to try to perceive patterns in the chaos.

Malkiel reports…

> "One chart showed a beautiful upward breakout from an inverted head and shoulders (a very bullish formation). I showed it to a chartist friend of mine who practically jumped out of his skin. 'What is this company?' he exclaimed. 'We've got to buy immediately. This pattern is classic. There's no question the stock will be up 15 points next week.' He did not respond kindly when I told him the chart had been produced by flipping of a coin. Chartists have no sense of humour."

Clearly, this chart tells us absolutely **nothing** about what the next coin toss will be, but our ability to spot patterns and create narrative can convince us that we have found something important. Now, I don't believe that business success is purely down to random chance; however, I do question whether we are as good as we think we are at spotting and deciphering the data that we have about businesses. We must acknowledge that an expert chartist can impose a narrative where none exists. How easy must it be for us to latch on to the wrong narrative in the complex and changing world of business.

Null Findings And Replications – Good Science But Not Good Stories

In 1989, Martin Fleischmann and Stanley Pons announced that they had successfully conducted experiments in cold fusion. Their apparatus of heavy water and palladium had apparently generated "excess heat"; in other words, more energy was coming out than was being put in. Their findings appeared to be due to some kind of nuclear fusion that was taking place at near room temperature. If they were right, it would have been a revolutionary moment for mankind and a potential source of limitless, cheap energy. Immediately after their announcement, laboratories around the world set up the same apparatus and tried to replicate their findings. One by one, they reported that they couldn't reproduce the same effects and, reluctantly, attention turned to what methodological failures may have accounted for the Pons and Fleischmann data.

This is how science works. If a finding is real, it should be possible to replicate the finding again and again. The cold burden of proof enables hard sciences to continue to progress and for the discoveries of some to be built upon by others. Unfortunately, in the "social" sciences, like management, things are not quite so simple. Social sciences rarely have definitive, repeatable cause and effect reactions; instead, a finding will tend to say that a certain input leads to a certain output more often than you might expect by chance. I won't bore you with the maths here, I will save that for Chapter 6, but the net result is that, in the study of anything to do with people, you are playing with probabilities.

Let me give an example of the kind of thing that a typical social science experiment might be able to reasonably say. A decent study could easily conclude that <u>client focus</u>, as measured by response times to customer queries, accounts for 10% of the difference in a business' profit. To back this up, the study would also say that there is only a 1 in 20 chance that this change to business profit was actually just a random occurrence and nothing to do with client focus (this is a standard benchmark used in many texts). In other words, the researchers would say, "We can't say that profit is all about customer response times but it appears to be a big contributor." Now the authors would acknowledge that they can't be 100% sure of this finding, as they haven't looked at every company in the world. However, through careful use of statistics, they can be 95% sure (that is 19 times out of 20) that it isn't just luck.

It is very easy for people to then take such findings and build further on them. Indeed, most texts will have reams of references at the end, quoting sources such as this in a way that makes them proof – in a way that makes them fact, but are they really? Well, maybe, but in order to be sure, I believe that there are two important things that should be more prevalent. Unfortunately, these things rarely happen, quite simply because they don't make a good story.

The first thing that should happen is that null findings should get reported. A null finding is an experiment that has failed to show an effect. It isn't an experiment that has demonstrated that there is no effect, rather it is one that has failed to provide sufficient evidence that there is one. A null finding may actually mean that there is no effect, but it could equally mean that there was not enough data, or the measurement approach was too crude, or some other methodological imperfection. As a result, null findings are not very interesting; they are not a good story, so they rarely get told. However, they do have an importance to social science. Look back at my example; I suggested that there was a 1 in

20 chance that my findings were actually just random. What you don't know is how many other things I have tried, how many other variants of the same question have been attempted. I may have asked the "client focus" questions in 20 different ways over the past year, but I am only reporting the one that gave me an effect – an effect that had only a 1 in 20 chance of being random. It is a bit like throwing a thousand dice on the floor and hunting around for patterns. You eventually find one cluster of dice that has neatly landed in order 1, 2, 3, 4, 5, 6 and then write that up as proof that when dice are thrown down, they like to arrange themselves in order. Ignoring the rest of the dice is like ignoring all the null findings.

The second thing that should happen is to conduct replications to validate findings, as was done in the cold fusion example. If an effect is true then another researcher in another part of the world, doing the same thing, should get similar results. Replication studies in leadership books have two distinct problems however. Firstly, real businesses aren't laboratory rats that can be easily manipulated. It is hard to say, find another ABB and do this to the leadership. The other problem is that they just don't make good stories. I replicated the same study as the last person and found the same thing doesn't get the pulse racing, and so rarely finds its way into print. People want a good story, and that means they want a new story, not a retelling of the old one.

In summary, there appears to be a conflict between good stories and good science. It is almost impossible to have a truly accurate and replicable insight into business that fits neatly into the simple narratives that we love. We therefore need to be conscious of which one we are reading, story or science. There is nothing wrong with leadership stories and parables, provided we realise that that is what they are. Likewise, there is a place for serious academic research, but it is in danger of being squeezed out of even academic publications because, truth be told, it is often a bit dull and modest in its findings.

Is Psychology The Worst Offender?

I fear my own particular leadership discipline of psychology may be one of the worst offenders. We seem particularly prone to these issues. In January 2013, *The Psychologist* magazine reported on the on-going issues of lack of replication in the discipline. They reported the conclusions of Harold Pashler and Christine Harris:

> "Assuming that 10 per cent of effects that researchers look for actually exist, that psychology experiments have an average power of 80 per cent to detect these real effects (which 'likely exceeds any realistic assumption'), and that all positive findings are published, the pair estimate that around a third of supposedly positive results reported in psychology could be false."

Not only might one third of results be false, but these results will likely be quoted in countless other articles and experiments, as scientists try to build on each other's findings. Given how many citations are included in every publication, it seems to be that virtually every paper written in my discipline may either be false, or at least cites another paper that is false as true. Less "standing on the shoulders of giants" and more "building on sand".

To make matter worse, *The Psychologist* also reported in October 2012 on the prevalence of a certain statistical finding. I mentioned before the 1 in 20 chance, which finds expression in psychology as something called p < 0.05. If a study can meet this hurdle, it is deemed fit for inclusion in journals. It seems that a deep study of papers published in a 12-month period from 2007-2008 found an anomalous bump of studies that only just made this benchmark, leading researchers to conclude that many studies that just fail to make the grade are being massaged over the line with some dubious techniques.

In other words, the failure to report replications and null hypotheses isn't bad enough; people are probably cheating to make results look real. They are doing so because they know that novel findings get published, so if they can't find one, they had better make one up, or at least bend the numbers a little in order to get published.

How Much Of Our Communication Is In The Words?

If, like me, you attended a management or leadership course at any point in the 90s, at some point, you are bound to have seen the trainer leap to the flip chart and ask, "So what percentage of our communication do you believe is in the actual words we use and how much is non-verbal?" After taking guesses, the trainer would have then delightedly revealed that only 7% is in the words themselves and a whopping 93% is non-verbal. Most people hearing this figure are sceptical, but the trainer would always point to the fact that this figure had been scientifically proved and you had therefore better pay attention to the rest of the course to make the most of the other 93%.

Of course, you will have probably guessed that this so-called fact is wrong and yet, it came to appear in almost every course I attended. Even now if you Google "non-verbal communication percentage" and look at the images, you will still find an abundance of pie charts demonstrating this "fact". It first came into existence following studies in the 1960s by Albert Mehrabian, who conducted two experiments. In the first experiment, subjects heard a voice saying "maybe" in three different ways and saw pictures expressing three different emotions. Picture seemed to convey emotions better than the voice tone. In the second experiment, subjects heard a total of nine words said in three different ways. Saying these words (e.g. "thanks") with a different tone of voice made a bigger difference to your perception of what the speaker was feeling than changing the word itself. He combined the data from these two studies to come up with the 7% figure. So there you have it, if you are only saying one word, then the way you say it and the look on your face is much more important than the word itself. In the real world though, we tend to say more than one word, so the 7% figure is ludicrous, and yet it was still used for decades. Why? Because it was memorable, it told a good story, and, more importantly, it told the story that the trainer wanted – "Pay attention to this course, what we are going to study now is really important and may even be the secret to great communication."

Don't Mistake Stories For Science

In this chapter, we have explored the stories that get told by gurus. We have found that these stories are either sanitised puff pieces of success, written by consultants, academics or journalists who are limited in their ability to criticise their sources or access data to get the full picture, or they are post-failure disaster stories, written with the benefit of hindsight and an edge of bitterness. We have also found that they are traditional stories that follow centuries' old traditions of storytelling, be it rags to riches or fatal flaws. The true facts are probably massaged into a satisfying and familiar narrative.

So does that make them worthless? The quote at the beginning of the chapter is from the author of *One Flew Over the Cuckoo's Nest* – *"To hell with facts! We need stories!"* Maybe he is right, we do need stories. It is how we think and how we learn. Perhaps our gurus are doing the right thing in packaging up learning about the world into neat, little stories. They are memorable, they are evocative, and they inspire action. Some CEOs will even hire professional storytellers to help them tell a more emotionally engaging story. The June 2003 issue of *HBR* included an interview with Robert McKee, a Hollywood screenwriting coach. In the interview, he describes the structure of a story that he would use to help a CEO engage with the emotions of his or her people.

"Essentially, a story expresses how and why life changes. It begins with a situation in which life is relatively in balance: You come to work day after day, week after week, and everything's fine. You expect it will go on that way. But then there's an event – in screenwriting, we call it the inciting incident – that throws life out of balance. You get a new job, or the boss dies of a heart attack, or a big customer threatens to leave. The story goes on to describe how, in an effort to restore balance, the protagonist's subjective expectations crash into an uncooperative, objective reality. A good storyteller describes what it is like to deal with these opposing forces, calling on the protagonist to dig deeper, work with scarce resources, make difficult decisions, take action despite risks, and ultimately discover the truth. All great storytellers since the dawn of time – from the ancient Greeks through Shakespeare and up to the present day – have dealt with this fundamental conflict between subjective expectation and cruel reality."

So stories do matter, and the guru books are a wonderful source of them. We can use stories to clarify a change that we need to make in our businesses, to bring it to life in a way that simplifies and engages. We can use stories to inspire people, to motivate people and give them the courage to act. Personally, I love to use stories and equally love to read the simple narratives that they provide. They are a great engagement tool.

The problem for me is that the stories we use are potentially wrong or incomplete. And if I literally and simplistically follow their advice, I am likely to make a mistake. When the ghostly voice of Obi Wan Kenobi says, "Use the force, Luke", I know it is fantasy. I may take out of it some confidence to trust in my own intuition and abilities, but I don't believe I have telekinetic powers. However, when a guru tells a story of a CEO who bets his company on a single product and succeeds, might there be a danger of the reader taking it as a genuine lesson that single-minded strategies are the best, not realising that there were many other things that led to the success of that decision that were not mentioned by the guru because they did not fit the narrative, and not realising that the leader who did the opposite and diversified also succeeded, and others who had taken either route had failed? We must remember therefore that these stories are stories and not recipes for success that can be neatly followed. The great thing is that there are stories in abundance so it is possible to find the one that matches what you wish to do with your business and you can use those stories to explain the plan and motivate the troops. Just don't, I beg you, use them to set the strategy for you. In being your own guru, find and tell the stories that matter to you and use them for what they are: an engagement device, not a panacea.

P.S. I Need A Hero

I am sitting on my desk on 12th January 2015, having just received an article from a former colleague who is interested in my work. The pivotal date of this article is 12th January 1942 – exactly 73 years ago today. My former colleague is Rob Morris, now a highly successful business psychologist, but one-time infantry officer and trained airborne ranger who instructed officer candidates at West Point. Rob has sent me the article following our conversation about the need for narrative, and he cited to me the example of US hero, Sandy Nininger – the first recipient of the Medal of Honor in World War II. While he became a byword for heroism during that period, and has had schools, ships and awards named after him ever since, Sandy was a somewhat unlikely hero. He was generally middle of his class at West Point and spent most of his time there in the library or at the theatre. However, his eventual heroism is evident from his Medal of Honor citation, the date of which had caught my eye:

"For conspicuous gallantry and intrepidity above and beyond the call of duty in action with the enemy near Abucay, Bataan, Philippine Islands, on 12 January 1942. This officer, though assigned to another company not then engaged in combat, voluntarily attached himself to Company K, same regiment, while that unit was being attacked by an enemy force superior in firepower. Enemy snipers in trees and foxholes had stopped a counterattack to regain part of their position. In the hand-to-hand fighting which followed, 2d Lt. Nininger repeatedly forced his way into the hostile position. Though exposed to heavy enemy fire, he continued to attack with rifle and hand grenades and succeeded in destroying several enemy groups in foxholes and enemy snipers. Although wounded 3 times, he continued his attacks until he was killed after pushing alone far within the enemy position. When his body was found after recapture of the position, 1 enemy officer and 2 enemy soldiers lay dead around him."

During his time at West Point, Rob Morris had had the opportunity to research Nininger. He painstakingly read through the previously unread archive of all Nininger's letters and other effects gathered before and after his death. Sandy Nininger was, it seems, a very unlikely hero, and was not particularly recognised as a leader before that fateful day. Notwithstanding the obvious valour described above, why was this previously very ordinary person chosen to epitomise heroism for a generation? Rob's answer is simple: It was because America needed a hero. The war had just begun and a previously sceptical public now needed to be engaged. As we have surmised, every engaging narrative has a hero. Many other heroic soldiers died after Sandy, but their names are largely forgotten, proving that the emergence of one special hero is as much about our need for one as their uniqueness. They have an important role to play in making sense of our world and uniting people, but we need to recognise that they are symbols, rather than undisputed truths.

Conclusion

Business writing seems to owe as much to fiction as it does to fact. Our brains seemed to be hard-wired for a story, so it is natural to make use of that fact to engage the reader. The problem comes when we are trying to discover the whole messy truth. If it doesn't fit a tight narrative structure then we may never hear it, even though it is vital to our business success. We also tend to play up the role of the hero of the story, someone we can look up to, admire and emulate. By the same token, we also seem to need a villain, someone to vilify and blame. For example, we could all take our fair share of blame for the Financial Crisis through our overuse of debt, but how much more comforting is it for us to construct a narrative that identifies and blames a few key figures at the top, especially if they happen to have a salacious backstory about drugs and prostitutes.

References

Booker, Christopher (2004) *The Seven Basic Plots: Why We Tell Stories*

Kelly, Christopher (2014) *Failings in Management and Governance: Report of the Independent Review into the Events Leading to the Co-operative Bank's Capital Shortfall*

Malkiel, Burton G. (2012) *A Random Walk Down Wall Street*

Wells, John R. (2012) *Strategic IQ: Creating Smarter Corporations*

Chapter 2
Playing Chicken With A Cliff:
Why Past Success Doesn't Always Predict Future Success

"Prediction is very difficult, especially if it is about the future."
Niels Bohr

"Everything will be all right in the end… if it's not all right then it's not yet the end."
The Best Exotic Marigold Hotel

Founded in 1931, national flag carrier airline, Swissair, was an amazing success story for many years. It was so effective at flying lucrative routes that it became known as "the flying bank". In the 1990s however, it looked like it was going to take this established success to even greater heights as it embarked upon its "Hunter Strategy", with the advice of world-leading management consultants. It aimed to grow its market share by embarking on a huge buying spree of smaller airlines. A decade later, the airline was stretched to the limit financially and questions were being asked, but before an adequate response could be implemented, the September 2001 attacks took place and the airline was doomed.

One of the built-in expectations that we seem to have is that any positive trend that exists will continue. If something is working, we expect it to keep working, and maybe even improve. In 1990, the leaders of Swissair mostly have looked back proudly on years of financial stability, and ahead optimistically about the great plans that they had. We may well expect a period of suffering to eventually end, but for some reason, we tend to assume that a period of success will continue. But how reasonable is that expectation in business? As we power our organisations along, do we face ahead of us an unlimited freeway, or are we actually hurtling towards a cliff? I believe that one of the reasons that the business writers so often praise an organisation that then fails is that the cliffs are much more common than we tend to think. The Swissair story is not that rare. Take this example from *Surfing the Edge of Chaos*:

> "No illustration of how the landscape can change is more compelling than the recent example of Monsanto. The initial success with genetically improved crops (and the speed at which these innovations were adopted in the United States) catapulted the enterprise to a new peak – and inadvertently put it into the crosshairs of a public relations nightmare. Monsanto was their darling of Wall Street one day, the instigator of 'Frankenstein Foods' the next. How this turnaround emerged is illustrative of the cascades and avalanches that can occur in living systems.

"An unrelated crisis in Britain, triggered when tainted beef from France was found to be carrying an infectious agent that caused mad cow disease, led to several deaths. No links to biotechnology, genetically modified foods, or Monsanto were ever suggested or considered viable, but this threat to public health was not well managed by the British counterpart to the FDA. Adding fuel to the fire, European Union authorities, almost simultaneously, suffered a similar embarrassment when it was disclosed that health authorities knew about, but did not alert the public to, toxins in Belgian poultry products. The alarm that spread throughout Europe was intensified by a loss of public trust in the institution ostensibly responsible for protecting consumers. Opposition without the scientific community mounted. All prior assurances by these agencies were now suspect; notable among them were earlier assurances that genetically modified crops and foods were safe.

"In the face of this disruptive shift, Monsanto endured a 20 per cent decrease in its market value and was eventually forced to merge with Upjohn to form Pharmacia."

Cliffs Happen... A Lot

If you take a long-term perspective of business, you will quickly see just how mortal most organisations are. Indeed, the average lifespan of an organisation is actually getting shorter. Erik de Haan and Anthony Kasozi (2014) report:

> "The average lifespan of large corporations has reduced by some 75 per cent over the past 50 years: the average lifespan of S&P 500 largest corporations in the US was more than 60 years in 1957 and is only around 15 years now. That means that looking ahead from 2014, it is likely that three quarters of the leading corporations on the S&P 500 will not exist in 2028."

Interestingly enough, when I joined the workforce back in 1991, people still talked about a job for life, but STC (the company that sponsored my PhD and offered me a job) ceased to exist as soon as I joined and instead, I was employed by Nortel, which is now dead too. Organisations have a shorter existence than a typical working lifespan, but we like to think of them as huge, indestructible edifices.

If you were to compare the Fortune 500 lists from 1955 and 2011, you would find that only 67 companies appear on both lists. In other words, less than 14% had managed to keep existing, or at least stay in the top 500 over that period of time.

Given this very limited lifespan, perhaps it should be no surprise to us that many businesses that were praised in the 90s are no longer with us, and perhaps we shouldn't criticise the gurus for that fact. In addition, these firms might not have shown many signs of their imminent demise. Businesses don't necessarily age gracefully and fade away, it is often much more sudden.

As John Wells says in *Strategic IQ: Creating Smarter Corporations*:

"Successful firms fail all the time and they fail dramatically. It is a common pattern: years of stellar profit growth and then sudden collapse. It does not appear to be confined to particular sectors or geographies. It happens to high-tech firms and low-tech firms, manufacturing businesses and service businesses, across all sectors of the economy and all around the world; it seems to be part of the price paid for success.

"A closer look at these failures suggests that they were self-inflicted. The victims did not adapt to a changing competitive environment. They succumbed to the fatal disease of inertia. As Jack Welch, former Chairman of General Electric, once said: 'I'm convinced that if the rate of change inside the institution is less than the rate of change outside, the end is in sight. The only question is the timing of the end.'

"Like many fatal diseases, this one can be slow to incubate. Sales and profits may continue to grow for many years after the initial inflection, lulling the firm into a false sense of security while it hurtles towards a precipice. By the time the organization is looking over the cliff at the rocks below, it is too late – the firm's fate is sealed. Companies with many years of financial success under their belts might do well to ask, 'Are we already dead?'"

The world of business also has its own unique way a creating a dramatic and sudden lifecycle – *the bubble*. Whether it be the Tulipmania of 1634-37, the South Sea Bubble of 1720, or more recent over-exuberance, it is easy to for us to get excited about a business or concept that has little intrinsic value, convince ourselves of its worth, and then come down to earth with a massive bump.

In the midst of all this stock market speculation are leadership experts who are looking for examples of success. I have often seen CEOs have their leadership approach praised on the justification of the way in which they have increased share price. If this price has been built on unwise speculation rather than good leadership, the lessons learned are unlikely to be of any use.

We can all look back with hindsight at these events and convince ourselves that we know the difference between market overconfidence and true value, but history suggests that the experts of the past have got it wrong, so it is arrogant to assume that we won't too. In the run-up to the Wall Street Crash, the highly respected Professor Irving Fisher of Yale offered his famous opinion that stocks had reached what appeared to be a "permanently high plateau", which, to me, just goes to prove how hard it is to differentiate a plateau from a cliff edge.

The Immortality Delusion

The Shelley poem right at the start of this book describes the ruins of the statue of the once great King Ozymandias. You feel the power of the empire that has been lost through his "sneer of cold command" and can only imagine the greatness of his kingdom. Like you, perhaps, I am reminded of the great edifices of our corporate kingdoms. I have frequently entered the head offices of mighty global corporations and been impressed by the scale and grandeur of the building; here, a ludicrously expensive sculpture, there, a deep mahogany desk overlooking a "power-view". The solidity of the construction stone is designed to make you feel the strength and permanence of the organisation housed within. It is desperately hard to think of these businesses as fragile or vulnerable, and yet, they must be, given their habit of suddenly dropping dead. Perhaps it is because the declines are so sudden that it is hard for us to see their fragility beforehand. It is therefore easy to praise, admire, write-up and try to replicate a seemingly strong business without really knowing how strong it is.

I have also found a number of business or industries that seem to be great at seeing the mortality of others, but have convinced themselves that they are an exception to the mortality rule. For example, it was very easy for big banks to consider themselves "too big to fail". They assumed that their importance to the economy was so great that any government would come in and bail them out if things went wrong. Of course, this has proved to be true for some, and has promoted much conversation about the "moral hazard" that ensues. If you really will be rescued when things go wrong, there is no disincentive to taking silly risks. However, the scale of the crisis meant that bailouts didn't save them all, and next time round, the safety net may be taken away.

Another recent example relates to tabloid newspapers in the UK. I have worked with more than one organisation of this type and remember very vividly one exchange that I had with a journalist. I was trying to make the point that poor values behaviour was being commercially punished in a range of industries, from supermarkets to coffee shops, from big pharma to high fashion, and that even if consumers didn't get upset, regulators would likely intervene. I was urging him to clean up his act before having to pay the price. His reply astounded me: "They will never dare take us on Paul. Every government knows that they need us to keep them in power, so they will never allow anyone to take us on." He clearly believed that the rules didn't apply to him or his industry. Too late the newspapers discovered that there was a line that even they could not cross, and the fallout continues to this day.

The Indicator That You Are Tracking Can Mislead You

Sometimes the cliff takes us by surprise because it is such a sudden and unpredictable event, but often, it is because we have been monitoring the wrong numbers. We have been watching one nice, steady, regularly climbing graph without noticing that another measure is heading the wrong way. We may be seeing sales grow, but do not notice that customer satisfaction is falling, for example. In today's sophisticated companies, it is rarely that simple of course, as nearly all businesses monitor a "balanced scorecard" of measures. However, the recent crash has thrown up some interesting other ways to look at indicators.

Take, for example, the recent issue of banking scandals. We have repeatedly seen that historic miss-selling of products to banking customers is now being paid for. How can we prevent this kind of thing happening in the future? Well, one school of thought is that we should start measuring "lead" rather than "lag" indicators. Lag indicators start to show a turn after you have done something wrong. Lead indicators are the signs that can be looked for before it is too late. The ultimate lag indicator of miss-selling is the rate of upheld complaints about a product being miss-sold. An earlier lag indicator might be spotting a sudden rise in complaints about a product. However, an interesting lead indicator might well be a sudden increase in profitability of a product, or an unexpectedly high number of sales. These latter two might normally be celebrated by a business, but perhaps they should be looked upon with caution instead.

In his book, *The Management Myth: Why the Experts Keep Getting it Wrong*, Matthew Stewart gives a particularly amusing example of a lead indicator:

> "One analyst shows that a good way to predict stock market movements is to track the percentage of Harvard Business School graduates who accept jobs in finance: if the number is below 10%, good times are ahead; if it exceeds 30%, a crash is looming."

Our problem of knowing which trend to track is made worse by the fact that businesses are artificially manipulating their numbers in order to reassure stock markets. As the markets do not like surprises, CFOs will always strive to keeps things as smooth and predictable as possible. So what gets reported and studied by gurus around the world is not always a true representation of what is actually happening.

Do Trends Continue?

The overall reason why businesses and people hurtle towards cliff edges in an apparently unknowing way is our belief in trends and the fact that they will continue. We tend to believe that the future is a continuation of the past. One repeatedly hears comments in the news along the lines of "... if current trends continue...". We use these trends to plan all manner of investments in the future – new school building, road and house construction, to name a few. Clearly, the analysis of trends is vital to our society. The problem is that they don't always make much sense. Take this example from Malkiel's *A Random Walk Down Wall Street*. If you look at the population trends for both the USA and the state of California, and then project them forwards, you will find that at some point they cross. If this were true then 120% of the population of the country would be living in California by 2045.

Obviously, we can't project too far ahead in our trends or one ends up with ridiculous answers like the one above, but surely, more immediate, short-term trends have validity? What about a team or a player who is on a winning streak in basketball? Let's look again to Malkiel for some information.

"In describing an outstanding performance by a basketball player, reporters and spectators commonly use expressions such as 'LeBron James has a hot hand', or 'Kobe Bryant is a streak shooter'. Those who play, coach, or follow basketball are almost universally convinced that if a player has successfully made his last shot, or last few shots, he is more likely to make his next shot. A study by a group of psychologists, however, suggests that the 'hot hand' phenomenon is a myth.

"The psychologists did a detailed study of every shot taken by the Philadelphia 76ers over a full season and a half. They found no positive correlation between the outcomes of successive shots. Indeed they found that a hit by a player followed by a miss was actually a bit likelier than the case of making two baskets in a row."

It seems that we have a natural tendency to believe in the predictive power of a winning streak, even when it is demonstrably not the case. I therefore believe that we often have too much belief that a company that has succeeded in the past has the recipe for success that will allow them to succeed in the future, just as we believe that a sports player might be on a winning streak.

Bringing this back into the world of business once more, we can see lots of evidence that past performance is a surprisingly inaccurate predictor of the future. We look to recent successful companies as a guide to future success, but even at the most basic level, this appears to be an error. If we wished to predict which business will grow well over the next decade, wouldn't we want to look carefully at the great successes of the past decade? They presumably have "the right stuff" and are worth a bet. Surprisingly, perhaps, it seems that the last people to bet on might be the ones who grew well in the past. Past earnings' growth actually doesn't predict the future growth. Looking at the growth rates of companies in one decade does not allow you to accurately predict which companies will be high growth in the next. We may feel as if it should, but the reality is that it doesn't. In fact, if you want to know which businesses will grow over the next decade, you are completely wasting your time betting on the success stories of the last decade.

External Forces

So I have established that businesses are far from immortal and indeed, it is quite likely that ones whose numbers seem good now might actually be heading for a cliff edge. And so business writers that use these companies as role models for us to follow may be making a mistake. However, these companies are generally staffed by very able people, apparently doing all the right things. Why then is there such a high chance of failure? Part of the problem appears to be that we have a delusion of control. As leaders, we believe that we can determine the success or failure of our businesses with some kind of agency. And while this must partly be true, it is also true that there are many other forces at play beyond our own willpower and decision-making. The strength of some of these forces can easily overwhelm a business, and it is often these forces that determine whether or not any particular business survives, no matter how compelling or brilliant the CEO at the helm is.

One way of looking at these forces is to consider Michael Porter's book, *Competitive Advantage*, which describes the five forces influencing profit in a business:

1. **Rivalry with existing competitors** – In my work, I have the fortune to work with many organisations that are in competition with each other. I have worked with nearly every bank in the UK, most of the insurance companies, and countless retailers. I have seen nearly all of them striving for excellence in leadership and management. In doing so, I see them reading the same books, consulting the same gurus, hiring the same management consultants, and even headhunting the same people. They even are often pursuing the same strategies and have identical market share increasing aspirations. They cannot all succeed in these aspirations, but they might all be trying to do so in the same way. It is easy to find the winners and ask them what they did to win, but I am fairly sure that the losers were trying to do the same thing too.

2. **Threat of new entrants** – If it wasn't bad enough that your existing competitors were out there fighting against you, new ones are always emerging. New entrants always have the advantage that they can adopt a brand new business model that exploits a weakness in the existing system. For established business to adapt to these new models may require

nearly impossible business transformation. The speed with which these new entrants can disrupt the market is devastating. Take, for example, the arrival of discounters, Aldi and Lidl, in the UK grocery market. The market was dominated by big supermarket brands that ran incredibly well-oiled machines. Tesco was praised for many years as being the master of this business, but excellent competitors like Sainsbury's kept them on their toes. However, when discounters arrived with much more limited product ranges, but at lower prices, they did so at just the right time, as the economy was struggling and people had become much more price-conscious. In the four years to 2014, the discounters doubled their share of the UK market.

3. **Threat of substitute products or services** – While the discounters shocked the supermarket business in the UK, at least they were selling broadly the same products. Sometimes, the force at play challenges the very existence of the product that you are selling. New technology is the source of countless examples of this type of challenge, whether it be vinyl replaced by CDs, CDs replaced by MP3s, or MP3s replaced by streaming – the threat of obsolescence is ever present.

4. **Bargaining power of buyers** – Another threat can occur within an existing business model that isn't bothered by such technological change. All it takes is for your success with one particular category of customers to become overdone into a problem. Many companies have been built off their

relationship to another business or small industry. Having the ability to manufacture a component for the latest technology can be a recipe for success. A business can grow rapidly if it is the only one that can provide the goods. Soon, of course, others will follow, and when that happens, your customer has choices and can begin to turn the screw. I know full well that purchasing departments have become more and more sophisticated and are often driven to meet extremely challenging financial targets; targets that can only be met by giving their suppliers less for more. They will quiz you about your accounts, crawl all over your business model, and find every opportunity to squeeze your margin to boost theirs. This can lead to bad outcomes for the buyers too, as they often destroy the quality suppliers and leave only the cheap, but that doesn't stop it from happening.

5. **Bargaining power of suppliers** – The reverse dynamic can be true when all the power is in the hands of the seller. You might think that such power can only exist if there is only one supplier of the desired product or service – an event that is rare and will not last long – but it can be subtler than that. Sometimes, while there are many other potential suppliers, the cost of switching is prohibitive. For example, if your business has built its entire infrastructure on one particular piece of technology, the supplier of that technology may start to increase licencing fees, knowing that the cost to you of moving your whole business may

mean you will tolerate their excessive terms for quite some while. While this will clearly impact profit, I have rarely seen this as such a "cliff-edge" situation as the other forces.

More recently, it has been suggested that there is a sixth force – complements. A complement is a product or service that works with your own product and service, and whose existence will either help or hinder you (e.g. music for your MP3 player or software for your hardware can either compete with your customer dollar or enhance it).

All six of these forces can have a sudden and unexpected impact on your business, no matter how customer-focussed, talented, lean and well-run it is. However, it would also be easy to say that the effective management of these forces is what sets apart a successful company from an unsuccessful company, and that the writings of the gurus and academics help us to do so better. In reality though, all too often, the success formulas that we are sold overplay the agency of the individual leader to navigate these forces and underplay how much of the success or failure of a business was down to forces beyond their control. It is easy to say "have the right product at the right time", "don't be dependent on any one buyer", "be flexible to new technology", but the reality is that the pace and size with which these forces act can overcome extremely well-run businesses, while at the same time, making heroes of others who, in reality, just got lucky.

So How Would You Know If You Were Heading For A Cliff?

Clearly, it is the case that we should treat some success stories that we read with care, as it may well be that the businesses we are reading about are, in actual fact, organisations that are heading off a cliff. But given the prevalence of such an event, wouldn't it be useful for leaders to know if they were in a similarly cliff-bound venture. Donald Rumsfeld once famously said:

> "Reports that say that something hasn't happened are always interesting to me, because as we know, there are known knowns; there are things we know we know. We also know there are known unknowns; that is to say we know there are some things we do not know. But there are also unknown unknowns – the ones we don't know we don't know. And if one looks throughout the history of our country and other free countries, it is the latter category that tends to be the difficult one."

While he was widely criticised for his lack of clarity, he did have a point that we could apply to organisations. The cliffs that we may be heading towards might fall into one of four broad categories, hinted at by Rumsfeld. There may be **known-known** cliffs, by which I mean that we know there is a threat to the business and we know the shape and size of that threat. There may be **known-unknown** cliffs, by which I mean that we know that the threat is ahead, but we don't know the nature of it. Obviously, there are **unknown-unknown** cliffs, where we are unaware of danger at all, let alone the nature of it. However, I also believe that there are **unknown-known** cliffs, which are threats that are known of somewhere in the organisational system, but do not have the attention of the people who matter. Some examples of these four cliff types are given in the table below.

	Unknown	Known
Known	We know our competitors are planning a new product, but have no details.	We know that if we can't get costs under control, we are doomed.
Unknown	A volcano grounds air freight for a year.	A technician in the business has spotted a major security risk but nobody is listening.

Awareness that the Cliff Exists (vertical axis)

Knowledge of the Cliff (horizontal axis)

Let us look in detail at each of these four cliff types.

Known-Known Cliffs

On first glance, these should be the easiest types of cliff to avoid, which makes one wonder why an organisation would be heading towards it in the first place. The reason will tend to be because of some new competitor or shift in the market. It is possible that some organisations are what John Wells refers to as "ostriches"; they see the threat and put their head in the sand for some reason. He states:

> "In the early 1990s, Circuit City, the leading US consumer electronics retailer, expressed concern each year in its annual report that aggressive discounters such as Best Buy were gaining share. They could see in published accounts that Best Buy's operating metrics, including sales-per-square-foot and sales-per-employee, were superior. But they stuck with their old model, expanding geographically and delivering growing sales and profits until they suddenly hit the wall and collapsed in 2001."

However, it is more likely that organisations are trying hard to avoid disaster, but the sheer mechanics of turning are difficult. An organisation may have legacy employees or infrastructure not suited to the new world. It may have a culture and competences that take time and skill to shift. It may lack the capital or shareholder will to invest in the necessary changes. However, the leadership will generally know the size and shape of the battle they are facing and will deploy the best response that can be mustered.

Known-Unknown Cliffs

The known-unknown cliff presents a problem. This is the type of cliff where you know that something threatening is looming, but you don't know the size or shape of that threat. If you don't know what exactly is ahead, how can you do anything about it? The answer will tend to be in making your organisation lean and adaptive. Whatever the threat, having control of costs, a flexible and skilled workforce, an outward-looking and customer-connected culture will all tend to enable you to see what is coming and make the necessary shift. Unfortunately, until the threat is real and tangible, any organisation finds it hard to commit the resources and effort required to create an agile organisation. Remember, they are still at this stage on the plateau. There are not yet the falling sales figures or other metric to spur us to action, so it would be easy to deprioritise the building of an adaptive and risk-aware organisation. It therefore needs leaders who will raise the potential cliff edge higher in the attention of their businesses and boards.

Unknown-Unknown Cliffs

Businesses are prone to rare, but high-risk events. Take, for example, the eruption of Iceland's volcano, Eyjafjallajökull, in 2010. While it had a significant impact on European business – I personally had to cancel a trip at that time – the eruption was short-lived enough to prevent too much permanent damage. However, back in 1821, the same volcano erupted for over a year. It could easily have done so again. Imagine how many businesses would suffer and potentially fail if that happened. True, some might maximise the opportunity (e.g. video-conferencing) but many more businesses that depend on air travel would run the risk of complete failure.

The insurance industry is, to some degree, designed around these low-frequency, catastrophic events, so many businesses keep well-covered. But there are other unknown-unknowns that no insurance policy is likely to cover; for example, the sudden invention of a new technology that renders your business obsolete overnight. Due to their very nature, it is hard for anyone to give advice on how to spot an unknown-unknown cliff, but we must always be aware that they exist. As financial service organisations are now very focussed on stress-testing their finances to ensure that they would survive the worst that the economy had thrown at them, they are like the people who build flood defences against the highest tide that anyone can remember, and then convince themselves that next time they will be ready. Unfortunately, in both cases, the past may prove an insufficient guide to the future, and the next time may be even worse than we imagine. Remember that the highest recorded tide was always higher than the previous highest recorded tide. The worst ever crash was worse than the last worst ever crash. Kidding ourselves into a false sense of security because we would be ready if the same event happened again is clearly misguided.

Unknown-Known Cliffs

The unknown-known cliff is an interesting challenge. Organisations are big and complex things these days and it is amazing how much knowledge there is in any business that is hard to access. What may, on first appearance, be unknown-unknowns are actually quite often known about by some people in the business well ahead of time. If only the right attention was given to the right facts, more cliffs might be avoided. In my experience, there are three reasons that this information does not get through.

1. **There is just too much of it to process** – So many people are raising so many red flags that it is impossible to sift through all of them. Like the secret services wading through millions of potential terrorist emails, it can be somewhat like spotting a needle in a haystack.

2. **No one is listening** – Some leaders lack the humility to listen to those who know. Quite often, the person who is raising the alarm is not the best or most respected communicator. Their motives are doubted, they are explained away as blockers, or they are just plain misunderstood. I find that some of the best-informed people about the threats to the organisation are often highly introverted, technical and non-managerial in nature. Their level of insight into the businesses is rarely matched by a similar level of influencing skill. As a result, they frequently become negative and resentful that nobody listens to them. These people are often thought of as Cassandras – the Greek princess cursed with never being believed. Ed Catmull, one of the founders of Pixar, has a much more interesting twist on this. It is not the Cassandra who is cursed; it is everyone else who fails to listen to her advice that is cursed.

"I spend a lot of time thinking about the limits of perception. In the management context, particularly, it behoves us to ask ourselves constantly: How much are we able to see? And how much is obscured from view? Is there a Cassandra out there we are failing to listen to?"

I frequently coach my clients to advocate on behalf of the Cassandras in their businesses. "Sure, they made their point in an overly negative, overly technical manner, but if you were trying to make the same point, how would you make it?" I ask. By answering this question, leaders often find their eyes opening to issues that they had previously dismissed. It is amazing how often the cliff ahead was well-documented, but somehow ignored. Take this insight from Pascale et al.:

"Consider IBM, which was one of the companies featured in *In Search of Excellence*. In 1993, Louis V. Gerstner, Jr, the company's new Chief Executive Officer, asked James Cannavino, a Senior Executive, to take a hard look at the strategic planning process. Why had IBM so badly missed the mark? Cannavino dutifully made his way through shelves of blue binders that contained 20 years' forecasts, trends, and strategic analyses.

"'It could all be stilled into one sentence,' he told Gerstner. 'We saw it coming... Our strategic planners foresaw the impact of PCs, open architecture, intelligence in the network, computers on microprocessors, even the higher margin of software and declining margins in hardware.' Pursuing the matter further, Cannavino turned to IBM's Operating Plans. Did they reflect the shifts the strategists had projected? These blue volumes could also be summarised in one sentence. 'Nothing changed.'"

3. **No one is talking** – There was for quite some time a management mantra that said, "Don't bring me problems, bring me solutions." Indeed, it was the mantra of the business world that I grew up in. I knew that if I wanted to impress my boss, she wanted me to show that I was a solution person, not a problem person. In the era of power-dressing and opportunity, it was essential to be seen as a "can-do" kind of guy. Unfortunately, this has led to a generation of managers who are reticent to bring concerns to bosses. They may fear that the messenger will be shot or at least disapproved of. Some of the ethical failure of recent years may have been less about bad people doing bad things and more about people trying to cope alone for too long. A recent client had a problem when a manager spotted an issue that would significantly impact profit. The manager concerned believed that if he escalated the issue, the first questions that would be asked were, "How big is the exposure?" and "What should we do to put it right?" The manager concerned therefore

spent the next month answering those questions so that he could impress his leaders with not only a problem, but also a solution. The sad reality was that this meant that the top of the business got to hear about the problem a month later than they should have. I therefore beg for a new risk-avoidant mantra: "Bring me the problems, we will figure out the solutions together."

A Quick Lesson About Influence

Early in my career, I used to run a course on influencing skills. This course was largely attended by people who had amazing ideas and intellect, but were unable to convince anyone else to listen to them. At the start of each course, I would put a sign up in the room that said:

Being right isn't convincing.

The problem that most of these people had was that they thought that having all the right arguments was all that you needed; they needed to accept that not everyone in the world is as logically driven as they are. However, I have recently come to another insight about influence, and that is:

Being convincing doesn't make you right.

The CEOs, journalists and gurus who offer us panaceas are all amazingly convincing; it is a shame that they are so rarely right.

Conclusion

So, what have we learned from this chapter? It seems that it is very hard to tell if you are on the open road, powering to more success, or heading for a cliff. Because of this, it is hard to know whether the successes of the past are good role models for the future. However, there is a glimmer of hope. If we stay alert to our own organisational mortality and the fact that cliffs surround us, we stand a chance of spotting them early and having an organisation that can turn or brake in time. Let us turn now to the person who is at the wheel and explore the compelling nature of CEOs.

References

Catmull, Edwin (2014) *Creativity, Inc. Overcoming the Unseen Forces that Stand in the Way of True Innovation*

de Haan, Erik and Kasozi, Anthony (2014) *The Leadership Shadow: How to Recognize and Avoid Derailment, Hubris and Overdrive*

Malkiel, Burton G. (2012) *A Random Walk Down Wall Street*

Pascale, Richard T., Middleman, M. and Gioja, L. (2000) *Surfing the Edge of Chaos: The Laws of Nature and the New Laws of Business*

Porter, Michael E. (2004) *Competitive Advantage*

Stewart, Matthew (2009) *The Management Myth: Why the Experts Keep Getting it Wrong*

Wells, John R. (2012) *Strategic IQ: Creating Smarter Corporations*

Chapter 3

The Smartest Guys In The Room:
The Compelling Nature Of CEOs

*"Here's to the crazy ones. The misfits. The rebels.
The troublemakers.
The round pegs in square holes.
The ones who see things differently.
They're not fond of rules. You can quote them,
disagree with them,
glorify or vilify them. About the only thing you
can't do is ignore them."*

Apple's "Think Different" Advertising Campaign

As business writers go about the task of seeking their formula of success, the first port of call is often the CEO – who better to ask about what has led a company to be successful than the person at the top? Journalists too love the opportunity to hear the secret of success from the great man or woman's mouth directly. Such appears to be the importance of these CEOs that they end up being our business celebrities and, increasingly, the heroes or villains of the unfolding business drama. As mentioned in Chapter 1, it is often the case that only the CEOs who are succeeding will be interviewed. Aside from the issues that this bias creates, this chapter will explore what it is like to meet these people and how their compelling nature makes them highly effective sales-people for their own approach. The question we need to explore is, just because they are compelling, does that make them right?

Spikey CEOs

Before getting into that question directly, it is also worth reflecting on the "spikey" nature of CEOs. They can simultaneously have very positive and negative behavioural tendencies, that figuring out what helps and what hinders their success can be a puzzle. Let me introduce you to two particular CEOs who have been well-covered by the press and gurus alike in recent decades.

RED PILL: THE TRUTH ABOUT LEADERSHIP

The table below contains a collection of quotes about each of them, made at their prime[1]:

CEO A	CEO B
From 2000 to 2008 he presided over his company's rise to global prominence as the world's largest company by assets.	His company gained 42% every year on average in stock valuation over the course of 14 years of his leadership.
The <company X> brand is now a worldwide presence.	In 2012 <company Y> became the most valuable company of all time.
He can't abide journalists.	He is cold and ruthless.
He is seen as a cold fish, a corporate Attila who isn't normal.	He is a demanding perfectionist.
He believes in the unfashionable concept of customer service.	His reinvigoration of <company Y> is one of the greatest turnarounds in business history.
He is fiercely driven and competitive, not given to small talk or frippery.	He is a charismatic and design-driven pioneer.
He prides himself on his decisiveness and his speed. He has a 'five-second rule', that his first instinct is the best.	He was named the CEO of the Decade by *Fortune* magazine.
He is *Forbes'* Global Businessman of the Year.	He has this very childish ability to get worked up about something... his way to achieve catharsis is to hurt somebody.
He generated a 27% rise in profits when the industry's global profits fell 30%.	He has been hailed as "a genius" and "the greatest CEO of his generation."
You sense he could tear you limb from limb, and you are ever so grateful when he doesn't.	He is rude, dismissive, hostile and spiteful.

---

1   CEO A quotes taken from *This is Money, Forbes* and *The Scotsman* between 2003 and 2005
   CEO B quotes taken from Walter Isaacson's biography of Steve Jobs

We seem to have here a description of two CEOs who contain large doses of both light and shade in their character. Neither sounds that much fun to work with, but both appear to achieve spectacular results. Or at least they did; in the period following these quotes being made, one went on to fail, and is regarded as one of the villains of the global financial crisis, and the other left us when he still seemed to have much more to give. CEO A is Fred Goodwin, the one-time CEO of RBS, and CEO B is Steve Jobs, who led Apple until 2011, when ill health prevented him from continuing. First off, before any reader explodes in outrage, I am not trying to equate these two very different people. I do, however, wish to explore the way in which we think about each of them, their strengths and weaknesses, in the light of their subsequent success or failure.

Fred Goodwin appeared to have performed a business miracle with Royal Bank of Scotland, which he took from being a small national to being the fifth biggest bank in the world through a series of ambitious acquisitions. However, in 2007, he engineered the takeover of Dutch Bank, ABN Amro, which was highly exposed to US subprime mortgages at exactly the wrong time. The subsequent disaster nearly brought down the bank, which was rescued by the UK Government, who took a 70% share. In the aftermath, many of the attributes described in the table were cited as reasons for his failure. His arrogant, bullying style was combined with his apparent ego and self-indulgence to explain what went wrong. Bizarre, but not necessarily true, stories were told about his determination to ban pink biscuits, and the alleged relocation of the executive kitchen to ensure that scallops were not cold by the time they reached him. We were led to conclude that these examples indicated the arrogance that contributed to the RBS woes.

By contrast, the more difficult sides of Steve Jobs' character have sometimes been used as an explanation for his success. Sure, he was demanding and punitive to those who let him down (he famously sacked the leader of the MobileMe team in public for failure), sure, he micro-managed every detail, but maybe that was why he got such great products. I recently attended a presentation by Ken Segall, the one-time ad agency Creative Director to Apple, who told us how he put the "i" into iMac. Ken was presenting his book, *Insanely Simple: The Obsession That Drives Apple's Success*. Within this book, he describes Steve Jobs' "rotating turret" thus:

> "... in some meeting, at some random time, some poor soul in the room would say something that everyone in the room could tell was going to light Steve's fuse.
>
> "First came the uncomfortable pause.
>
> "The offending comment would reverberate in the air, and it would seem as if the entire world went into slow motion as Steve's internal sensors fixed on the origin of the soundwave. You could almost hear the meshing of gears as Steve's 'turret' slowly turned towards the guilty party. Everyone knew what was coming – but was powerless to stop it."

Far from seeing this as a business-harming character flaw, Segall seems to link it clearly to what made Jobs and Apple so successful. He compares Dell to Apple. On the one hand, Dell spent excessive time producing documents to clarify what they stood for as a brand. Jobs kept Apple much simpler by using his "turret":

> "If anyone had asked him to hand over such a document... We might even have been fortunate enough to see his 'rotating turret' in action."

It seems that the RBS failure causes us to see Goodwin's quirks as the problem, but Apple's success as being supported by similar quirks. Is that true or is it an illusion? Imagine, if you will, a parallel universe. In this universe, the banking crisis does not happen and RBS goes on to be the biggest bank in the world. By contrast, consumers take one look at the iPad, shrug their shoulders and return to their laptops, leaving Apple in a terminal tailspin. In such a world, I firmly believe that the apparently awful elements of Fred Goodwin's style would be rationalised as part of what lead to his success. "Sure, he banished pink biscuits and moved the kitchen to ensure his scallops were warm, but that is the kind of perfectionism that makes a bank great," they would say. "So what if he spent £200m on celebrity endorsements, how do you think you are going to build a global brand?" By contrast, I can imagine the character assignation of Steve Jobs: "You can't run a successful business by being a bully and a control freak," they would claim.

It seems to me that it isn't the actual value of attributes of the individual that we are attending to, rather we are attending to success or failure itself then buying into the simple story that people who succeed are doing everything right and people who fail are doing something wrong. So when the gurus meet the CEOs who succeed, they try to list out and bottle the magic formula, even if in reality, it is laced with a dose of poison.

Angels And Demons

We do seem to like the idea of CEOs as heroes and villains; if you think of the big names in business of recent years, you will quickly put them into one camp or another.

In the course of my career, I have been fortunate enough to meet a number of famous CEOs, heroes and villains alike. Without naming names, let me give you a quick flavour of what two of them were like. Person A was one of the rudest I have ever met. Throughout our meeting, this person bounced a ball against the wall directly above my head, breaking off only to yell at people who were walking past the door. It was abundantly clear that this person was super powerful and I was powerless to resist. By contrast, Person B was charm personified – self-deprecating, funny and fascinating, I felt privileged to be in their company, yet treated as an equal for being there.

So which was the "villain" and which was the "hero"? Well, you will have read the press about both of them and probably concluded that they were morally responsible for some of the failings of their whole industries. However, at the time that I met them, both were on the road to becoming heroes and had yet to reach the peak of their careers. With the benefit of hindsight, I could sound wise in explaining their respective downfalls. I could paint an excellent picture for you of the personality traits of each and explain to you the deep psychology behind their eventual failure. But in all honesty, at the time, the only thing that was clear was that they were big characters, one a big bully and the other a big charmer. Sure, they both had flaws, but so has everyone that I have ever met. They also had amazing strengths; strengths that positioned them both at the top of challenging career ladders. I could pretend that my great insight allowed me to see through them. I have even gone through the notes that I took at the time and, sure enough, I referenced things that I could now proudly point to that and explain what happened to them. This would be a neat trick to massage my own ego, but I have identified strengths and weaknesses in everyone that I have met. Could I honestly say at the time that I knew which person's flaws would later be seen the same light as Fred Goodwin's are, and which ones would be looked back on with the same forgiveness (or even admiration) with which we view Steve Jobs? I confess I couldn't. Yet, over and over again, gurus try to do just that, to identify the winners and then praise all their traits, or name and shame the losers and condemn all theirs. The problem is in knowing who is the Angel and who is the Demon.

Why Even The CEOs Who Subsequently Fail Seem To Impress

Notwithstanding the ball-bouncing bully, the CEOs I have met have all impressed me. I haven't liked them all, but I cannot deny that they were impressive. It may be that I am easily impressed, but I was recently pleased to read a similar quote from Daniel Seligman, who wrote:

> "I spent some 40 years as a writer and editor of *Fortune* magazine and during that time I have met hundreds of CEOs. Not all of them proved entirely lovable, and some of them were not particularly interesting when asked for opinions on social or political issues remote from their business concerns. But I cannot recall meeting a CEO who did not come across as highly intelligent."

Maybe then it is their intelligence that is so impressive; let us take a look at that aspect of CEOs in more detail. The title of this chapter comes from the story of Enron, the leaders of which were dubbed "The smartest guys in the room" in the famous book by Bethany McLean and Paul Elkind. Clearly, they were doing something so impressively clever that it was hard to see that what they were actually doing was fundamentally wrong. People who didn't "get it" assumed that they themselves were wrong and that these smart people must know what they were doing. The intellectual prowess of the Enron leaders enabled them to create enough confusion and doubt in analysts, journalists and investors that they were able to go on the wrong path for a long time before anyone noticed. So, is this apparent intellectual superiority over all-comers the norm? In part, but not completely.

Various researchers have shown that IQ contributes to business success (Schmidt and Hunter, 1998).

Furthermore, it seems to matter more as you get more senior. Henry Thompson, in his blog, suggests that it is hard to rise up the corporate ladder unless your IQ is in the 120-125 range. Meanwhile, Jonathan Wai finds that 39% of Fortune 500 CEOs are gifted (IQ > 135). Although there are probably even higher proportions among university professors, it is still pretty impressive. Having said that, surely the various gurus who meet with these CEOs are batting in the same league so will not be easily bamboozled. Well, not necessarily; you see, it isn't all about raw IQ. The people also have a great deal of knowledge and experience to back that IQ up. If you spend all your time thinking about your business, if you have spent 20 or 30 years working in the same industry or even the same organisation, your raw intelligence is magnified by the insight that your career has given you. I may well have been smarter than some of the CEOs I have met, if you measure "smarts" by the ability to fill in IQ tests, but they have always left me standing when it comes to their knowledge of their business and market. This fundamentally means that my ability to spot the flaws in their arguments is seriously compromised and, while I can challenge and ask cleaver questions, at the end of the day, they will be able to win any business argument with me that relates to their own business. Knowing this, most business gurus will take as read the CEOs version of things. If a highly successful CEO explains to you the five reasons why they have been able to build success, the most obvious thing to do is write them down and say thank you very much. And if it doesn't seem to make sense, if you don't understand really how it works, then the obvious conclusion is that you are lacking in the intellect and insight to understand, not that they were wrong. After all, you only have to look at their results.

The subject of "results" is worthy of some consideration in its own right. It is certainly hard to disagree with someone who is succeeding, but let us pause and return to that issue later and continue now with other aspects of the personality of CEOs.

The Core Drive Of CEOs

So we know that CEOs are generally bright – sometimes, but not always, the brightest guys in the room – but it's not necessarily their smarts that have got them there. There is a lot else going on. In my role as a business psychologist, I get to interview huge numbers of senior leaders. I estimate that I have profiled 1500-2000 people so far. This profiling includes spending four hours with each person, speaking about their history and what has got them to the top. We start way back in the beginning with childhood and family, all the way through to the current role. Of my 1500+ interviewees, a few made it to middle management, most were senior management, and a good proportion of those were C-Suite. The stories that I have heard are wide-ranging and humbling to hear. People have shared with me the darkest moments in their lives with many tears through to tales of success, fame and fortune.

A recurring theme in the interviews of the most senior and successful is finding something that has acted as a source of huge amount of drive, something that spurs them on to try harder than anyone else. Some examples that I have heard include:

- Being small and bullied at school
- Having a disabled sibling who required most of the parental attention
- Having a distant or hard-to-please parent
- Loss of a parent or sibling
- Having a hugely famous or successful parent
- Having a parent face bankruptcy
- Being made a refugee

People who have experienced these things in early life often have a grit and determination that their peers lack. Their drive for love or fear of failure keeps pushing them on and finds expression in the workplace. They often fixate on career or financial success as the way of getting satisfaction – as a way of compensating for any inferiority that they may feel. However, the feeling often stays with them, even when they have achieved amazing success, and the resulting continual state of dissatisfaction keeps spurring them on. It is not enough to gain promotion, fame, riches or whatever once. They need to do it next year and the year after, to prove their value again and again. People with this huge level of drive will work longer hours, sacrifice holidays and family time. They will commit themselves completely to the task at hand. By contrast, I also see (normally at more junior level) people who are satisfied. They have a good job, they are well paid, and now they want to share their success with their loved ones. They will often tell me that they don't want to get promoted. They will say, "I look up at my boss and see what s/he has to do, the hours they work, the tough and aggressive way they have to behave, all of the politics, and to me, it just isn't worth it. Sure, I would like the kudos and extra money, but not that much."

More and more, I see that organisations are demanding a huge amount from their top people. If you are a CEO, everyone wants a piece of you: investors, the board, media, employees and customers. Anyone prepared to take on such a role needs some special kind of motivation. Many times, there is a noble motivation – to change to world, the industry or the company, but it is never a half-hearted motivation.

So why am I telling you all this? The reason to pause and reflect on the drive of these leaders is that they are totally committed to their businesses. They will eat, sleep and breathe the industry that they are in. Often every waking hour will be used by these people (who we have already established are bright) to understand and maximise the performance of their company. No matter how clever the guru or journalist who comes to quiz them, no matter how much prep they have done ahead of the meeting, the CEO will have done more. This level of drive will make them intensely compelling. Not only will the drive in itself impress, it will also lead to such a well-informed individual, that once again, it is hard to spot anything that they have not already seen and, in their own minds, at least resolved. They are believers, deeply committed to their cause; they could not operate without this sense of certainty and self-belief. When we meet a business leader who is clearly bright, has considered all the angles, yet seems deeply committed and believing, it is very hard to do other than assume that the model of success that they are espousing is the right one, especially if the business results are showing success.

I Believe In Me

Huge self-confidence runs in tandem with the drive of these leaders. This self-confidence often leads CEOs to believe that their success is due to their own special abilities much more than is the case. They attribute their results to something special about them and what they did, rather than to the huge range of other factors that may have been at play.

In his book, *What Got You Here Won't Get You There*, CEO Coach Marshall Goldsmith describes how delusional this self-belief can be:

> "In my career, I have asked 50,000 participants in my training programs to rate their performance against their peers. Eighty to eighty-five per cent of them rate themselves to be in the top twenty per cent. Seventy per cent declare themselves to be in the top ten per cent. If you shift the population to people with higher perceived social status, such as investment bankers, airline pilots, or doctors, 90 per cent of them place themselves in the top 10 per cent of their profession."

So it is not just CEOs – we all have a tendency to over-rate our own abilities and hence, probably our own contribution the success of our business. So if you ask people why they succeeded, they are almost certain to over-emphasise the things that they did as the root cause of that success. In his popular book, *Outliers: The Story of Success*, Malcolm Gladwell gives lots of examples of the other things that may lead to success beside personal brilliance. One particular example sticks in my mind; he provides a list of the 75 richest people of all time and finds that the Americans on the list were all born within a decade of each other – the 1830s. When looking at more up to date billionaires (including Bill Gates and Steve Jobs), he finds that, by-and-large, they were born between 1953 and 1956. Both cohorts were lucky enough to reach maturity at a time of huge economic opportunity, and were clearly talented enough to exploit that opportunity. There must have been equally talented people born outside these golden years, but we will never know their names. Would one naturally attribute the amazing success of these people to the year they were born? Of course not – we look to their hard work and stunning intellects. But, in reality, there must be so many other contributing factors they or we never perceive. The secret of my success may even be a secret from me.

The CEO As The Super Salesperson

The final trick that the CEOs have up their sleeves is an interpersonal one. No matter how bright and driven you are, you will never get to the top unless you can have influence over other people. As a result, the most senior players will generally be very interpersonally influential. I don't mean that they are all charming and charismatic, although many are. They may well be loud, aggressive and bullying, or even quietly intimidating. However, all of them have some interpersonal approach that allows them to gain the upper hand when working with others.

The most successful leaders have a combination of three things: a good degree of self-awareness, an ability to read the audience, and an adaptability of influencing style. If you know how you are coming across, can see how it is landing with others and can then shift approach accordingly, you will have a tremendously ability to influence others. In my experience, most top leaders do have these skills. You can only go so far on your own; eventually, you need to bring others with you. Perhaps this is why Microsoft CEO, Satya Nadella, has been widely reported as saying, "In the long-run, EQ trumps IQ."

Whether it be in intimate one-on-ones or rallying speeches to thousands of followers, the great CEOs tend to be great communicators, great influencers, great salespeople. So when they explain to you the reasons for their company's success, they will do it with all the skill that they bring to bear when negotiating with suppliers, briefing investors or talking to the press. They are schooled in the craft of delivering a message in a compelling way, and it is easy for them to be as compelling about profound truths as they are about misconceptions or illusions.

In smaller businesses, you may get away with less of these attributes; you have probably met plenty of people with CEO on their business cards who actually turn out to be the front person to someone else who is really the source of power. But at the level of the Fortune 500 or FTSE 100, this cannot be the case. To rise to the top of an organisation of 200,000 people requires more than having a face that fits. You need the ability to continually differentiate yourself against an ever-more challenging peer group and then win their followership as you rise above them. Believe me, top CEOs are pretty compelling characters – people with the ability to influence at such a degree that they can convince thousands of people of a decision that is often built on the flimsiest of evidence.

Putting It All Together Into A Compelling Package

It seems to me that the CEOs who we go to for advice have all three of these attributes of judgment, drive and influence in a high degree. Indeed, my former employer, YSC, use these labels in their highly-regarded Success Model. By spotting these attributes, it is possible to predict potential leaders of the future. Certainly, the ones who have made it seem to score well across this basket of measures. When put together, they make for a powerful combination. The CEO in front of me may or may not be as bright as me, but when combined with vast experience of and total immersion in his business, he will be a much better judge of his own business matters than I will ever be. He will be driven and committed to an extreme degree; the sheer passion, energy and hard work that this person will put into further building this understanding will always leave me behind. This person will also be interpersonally compelling, may be a bully who terrifies me into agreement, or a charmer who has me in the palm of his or her hand. Either way, I will find it hard to argue.

So when the researchers approach the CEO for the secret of his success, they will be faced with a truly compelling arsenal of influence. Furthermore, the successful CEO will also have that very success as an ace up the sleeve. You just can't argue with success, can you? Over and again, you will be confronted with the person who says, "This is what I did and this is what I have achieved. I must therefore be doing the right thing. If you want to succeed too, do what I am telling you." It does end up being quite a hard thing to argue against. However, there are two obvious problems with this – first, the success of today may be the failure of tomorrow. Just because I am trouncing competitors now, just because my share price is through the roof, it is only a moment in time and so may not predict future success. Secondly, even the successful CEO who stays successful may be mistaken about the reasons for their own success and so, once again, give you the wrong advice.

Did I Tell You About The Time When I Really Got It Wrong?

When I work with my clients, we tend to form a clear view of the culture of the business once we have assessed a dozen or so senior executives. We can begin to figure out why it is succeeding or why it is struggling. In the course of doing this over many years, I once had a very interesting experience. A colleague and I had spent a month with an amazingly successful business that was head and shoulders above its competition in virtually every business metric that you could think of, but something seemed a bit odd. This business appeared to have few good leaders, little in the way of values, some disdain for its customers, and a level of micromanagement that heaped pressure on all junior people. We wrestled with this paradox for a long time. We were both students of a more progressive philosophy of management – one that believed in leaders who had a compelling sense of purpose. We idolised those organisations that won the commitment of their people to a bigger cause and, in so doing, enabled the leaders to rise up and allowed the people below them to flourish. This client seemed to do none of these things. The moral compass was more than a little wonky and the leadership style was aggressive and controlling. When we mentioned our concerns, the HR Director neatly explained them away. We didn't understand the unique dynamics of this industry it seemed. My idealistic, tree-hugging philosophy didn't wash with these people, he explained. How else could we explain the huge success of this business? We were told that no one knew why this apparent dysfunction worked so well, but it clearly did, "so please don't mess with it". After lots of soul-searching, we had to come to the conclusion that we must have got it wrong. The things that we were convinced should lead to success did not appear to apply to this industry. We just couldn't effectively argue with results.

Quite a few years later, this business did meet with disaster. A disaster not unrelated to what we had seen, but for the period it succeeded, any attempts to critique were always met with the argument that nothing succeeds like success. I still kick myself when I think back on this incident. I was right in my concerns about this business; could I have done more to convince them? Perhaps I could, but I learned how hard it is to point to success and call it doomed. No one will listen and the balance of evidence is on their side. Imagine how hard it is to ever get such a story into print (before it is too late that is).

How CEOs Miss-Explain The Secret Of Their Success

What is interesting is how poor successful people can sometimes be at explaining the reasons for their success. They can remember some of what they have done, see the success that they have had, and conclude than one was the cause of the other. What they can never know is whether doing something else would also have succeeded to the same or better degree or whether doing the same thing in a slightly different context would have failed. They can also slightly miss-remember what actually happened. A common conversation that I have had with leaders over the years goes something like this:

Me: "Tell me about how you succeeded in turning that business around."

Leader: "Well, I sensed that something was wrong in our Luxembourg division, so I sent people down to check it out and they found that customer complaints were going through the roof. We tracked down the source of those complaints to quality control issues and putting that right had a transformational effect on profit."

Me: "So what has that taught you about what makes you successful?"

Leader: "It is customer focus, isn't it? You need to always stay close to how they are responding to your product."

A fairly clear-cut business lesson it seems, but on closer examination, you realise that this leader's customer focus wasn't the reason for their success; it was their ability to "sense" that something was wrong. It could equally well have been that costs had gotten out of control, or that employee morale was down – the leader didn't know till they looked into it – but with hindsight, the cause was obvious. When we look back at things, we see the path we took and the consequence of every action and decision, but it is often hard to remember what you actually thought or did at the time. It is hard to remember the luck that supported one course of action or to recall the other courses that could have been taken, which may have been equally successful. The problem with most CEO success stories is that they are written with hindsight where everything is clear and they sometimes reveal little of the messiness and unpredictability that was the reality at the time
   One of the exceptions to this self-deluding rule is Ed Catmull, one of the founders of Pixar. He has this much more honest self-reflection.

> "... a familiar, oft-repeated phrase kept popping in my head: 'Hindsight is 20-20.' When we hear it, we normally just nod in agreement – yes, of course – accepting that we can look back on what happened, see it with total clarity, learn from it, and draw the right conclusions.

"The problem is the phrase is dead wrong. Hindsight is not 20-20. Not even close. Our view of the past, in fact, is hardly clearer than our view of the future. While we know more about a past event than a future one, our understanding of the factors that shaped it is severely limited. Not only that, because we think we see what happened clearly – hindsight being 20-20 and all – we often aren't open to knowing more."

So Is It Just CEOs Who Are Compelling Yet Wrong?

It seems likely that this general effect of compelling CEOs will apply elsewhere. In essence, if you have a bright, driven and charming person who appears to be succeeding in whatever domain, then it is almost irresistible to ignore their rationale for their own success. Take the world of health and fitness. People who have committed themselves to a certain diet or exercise regime and are now the picture of health and fitness can easily sell their (sometimes literal) recipe to those who desire to emulate them. On the face of it, this is all very noble. "I have found the way and (for a modest fee) I am allowing you to do so too." The problem is that the successful person themselves may not actually understand the reasons for their own success. You see, we never get to hear the story of the person who apparently did all the right things, who ate the right food and played the right sport and yet, for reasons unknown, couldn't shed the pounds. We do, however, hear from the bright, driven and eloquent salesperson who can tell a compelling story behind their success. If challenged, they can always return to the statement that "you can't argue with results".

This phenomenon has been described by Francesca Gino in *Sidetracked* as outcome bias, and she provides us with an interesting experiment to make the point.

"Consider the following hypothetical scenario of a surgeon deciding whether or not to recommend a risky operation:

> "A 51-year-old man had a heart condition. He had to stop working because of chest pain. He enjoyed his work and did not want to stop. His pain also interfered with other things, such as travel and recreation. A type of bypass operation would relieve his pain and increase his life expectancy from 65 to 70. However, eight per cent of the people who have this operation die from the operation itself.
>
> "The decision of whether or not to recommend the surgery is obviously a difficult one for the doctor. What do you think he should do? You may be undecided, but keep reading.
>
> "His physician decided to go ahead and recommend the operation, and the patient went through with the surgery. The operation was a success.
>
> "Based on this information, how would you evaluate the quality of the surgeon's decision? Was the decision to recommend an operation the right one? Moreover, how competent do you think the surgeon is?

"Now consider a different version of the same scenario. The surgeon is faced with the same difficult decision. This time, however, you learn that the surgeon went ahead with the operation, but the patient died. In this case, how would you evaluate the equality of the surgeon's decision to recommend the operation? And how would you evaluate the surgeon's competence?"

When experiments are conducted that present these scenarios to people, there is a marked difference between how positively the decision-making of the doctor was viewed when the patient survived and how negatively it was perceived when the patient died.

The Sports Hero Story

There is one walk of life that is dominated by results: sport. And so it is no surprise that those who have achieved sporting greatness are revered and emulated. Biographies become bestsellers and pundits pore over the secret of their success. Like CEOs and gurus, they tend to reflect on their persistence, dedication and self-belief, which they combined with innate talents and attributes. The debate rages over which is more important: the talents they are born with or the practice that they put in. But it has to be one or the other, doesn't it? Well, maybe not. Take the story of Ed Smith, journalist and former England cricket player. He has written of his own adoration and emulation of a cricketing great from a former era, Geoff Boycott:

"Even as a child, I sensed there was something in Boycott that was different – an application of willpower, an elimination of error, an unbendingness and relentlessness... [I] stood in front of the television as a four-year-old boy, front forearm wrapped in a white paper bag to replicate the Boycott armguard, trying to emulate the great master's forward defence: implacable, controlled, defiant, solitary.

"It used to amuse me – much later, in the grown-up world – when sports psychologists told me to practise 'positive visualisation'. I'd been at it since I was four.

"My view was simple: if you had ability and you practised enough, nothing could stop you."

Ed indeed went on to succeed at the highest levels of the professional game, until an injury ended his career. This event caused him to re-evaluate his whole life in his book, *Luck*. It does not dwell on this piece of "bad" luck – the injury that ended his career; rather he explores all of the good luck that had enabled him to succeed before his accident. There were a whole range of factors in his life (luck, if you will) that enabled him to get to the top of his sport. However, it was only when his career was over that he was able to see clearly what was behind his success. If you had asked him at the time, he would have given the standard formula of practice and self-belief. We will explore more of this theme in Chapter 5, but the issue of the successful role model creating a misleading template of success is clearly an idea that can be extended to all walks of life.

Sport gives us a rich source of examples about how wrong people can be when it comes to discerning the root cause of their own success. In *Bounce*, Matthew Syed describes his journey to becoming the British number-one table tennis player:

> "But what made me special? What had marked me out for sporting greatness? I came up with a number of attributes: speed, guile, gutsiness, mental strength, adaptability, agility and reflexes."

> While these attributes intuitively sound reasonable explanations of his success, he then goes on to describe the many circumstantial conditions that enabled him to get the practice needed to get to the top. Even the street he was on appeared to confer some advantages:

> "For a period in the 1980s, this one street, and the surrounding vicinity, produced more outstanding table tennis players than the rest of the nation combined."

In the end, he concludes that:

> "If a big enough group of youngsters had been given a table at eight, had a brilliant older brother to practice with, had been trained by one of the top coaches in the country, had joined the only 24-hour club in the country, and had practised for thousands of hours by their early teens, I would not have been number one in England."

Just liked Ed Smith, Matthew Syed would, at the peak of his career, have given an entirely different explanation of his success to the one that he eventually arrived at late in life. Now it may be that the new interpretation is as wrong as the original one, but they cannot both be 100% true. What we can certainly learn is that the successful person is not the most reliable source of information on their own success.

What Lessons *Can* We Learn?

Surely, we can't just dismiss these great people as unreliable witnesses who can teach us nothing about the nature of their own success. No, we cannot ignore them, but if we are to find our way in the world of business, sport, politics or whatever, we must find a way of looking beyond the compelling nature of the messenger and strip away their many illusions:

- An intelligently-structured argument is not necessarily right.
- The commitment and belief of others to a solution is not necessarily an indication of its worth.
- A captivating influencer and charismatic speaker is no more right than the giver of a boring monologue.
- Successful people don't always accurately understand the reasons for their own success.

But this doesn't mean to say that there is nothing to learn from these great leaders – the ones that succeeded and the ones that failed. As the quote at the start of this chapter says, *"You can quote them, disagree with them, glorify or vilify them, but the one thing you can't do is ignore them."* We need to look beyond their own interpretations of their success, the hero worship or vilification of others, for a deeper insight. We need to find what resonates with us and our experience, to find our own voice, our own leadership signature. If we borrow from others completely, even if they are successes, they offer no guarantee of success to us, but these stories of CEOs do perhaps give us the courage to keep being the kinds of people that we want to be.

The Story Of Andy Briggs

Let me close this chapter by telling you about two CEOs who I have been fortunate enough to work with and who provide inspiration to me.

At the time of writing, Andy Briggs was the CEO of Friends Life, a FTSE 100 Life and Pensions company (he now leads the Aviva UK Life Business), but I had been lucky enough to have worked with him for a number of years preceding this and have come to admire him more with each passing year. The financial services industry has come in for a lot of criticism over recent years, and rightly so, but those of you who are close enough to it will know that it is still filled with decent people who are striving to do a good job for their customers. Andy is one of those people. He has always been hard-working and ambitious, but what has come much more to the fore as he has progressed is the purpose behind that ambition. You will frequently hear him describe Insurance as a "noble profession", a profession that exists to be there for people at the most challenging and difficult times of life. He takes his responsibility to society seriously and, as a parent of young children, you can see how he is striving for a better world for them. On top of this drive is a fierce intellect – he is incredibly sharp and has such experience of the industry that what he doesn't know about Insurance isn't worth knowing. One of his team recently complained to me that Andy knew more about the numbers than the people whose job it was to know about the numbers. Finally, he has an easy, down to earth and approachable style that allows him to win people over without pulling rank, while showing the confidence to make the decisions that are his to make. This wasn't all nice style and no substance, however; during his four years at the helm, he took a £3.4 billion business, returned £1.4 billion to shareholders and, when the business was sold, still ended with a valuation of £5.8 billion.

Andy is a model leader in my book and I would aspire to be like him, but does that guarantee success? Might a reader picking up this book in five years' time be able to say, "Him? Are you kidding? Look what happened to him." Maybe. I hope not, but yes, maybe. Being a great leader isn't a recipe for success. It should be, but it isn't. If he continues to succeed, I won't be more right in my admiration of him. If he fails, I won't be wrong in admiring those traits named above.

The Story Of Stephen Page At Faber

Another great leader I have worked with for getting on 20 years is Stephen Page, the CEO of Faber, the highly-respected, independent literary publisher with an illustrious, 80-year history of publishing major writers. Their authors include Poet Laureates, Nobel Prize Laureates, Booker Prize-winners and bestsellers. Literary publishing not an easy business to be in – the level of change is huge and generally negative. Bookshops are disappearing off our streets to be replaced by huge online retailers who use their size to demand low prices. Supermarkets stock a few bestsellers (again at low prices), leaving little market for books that aren't blockbusters. The financial security of publishers therefore becomes increasingly dependent on finding predictable "hits" rather than publishing challenging literature. In the midst of this, Faber stands as one of the last substantial independents against an army of giants. Like Andy, Stephen is a great intellect and his brainpower is oriented towards the literature he loves. Most conversations with Stephen will involve at least one cultural reference that goes soaring over my head. He also works hard at his thinking; on a number of occasions, he has told me of plans to work away from the office for a few days to think about the business. This makes him one of the most strategic people I have met. He is constantly looking at trends, predicting the future and positioning his business accordingly.

Stephen is also never satisfied, particularly with himself. He only has rare moments of feeling comfortable, before he turns once again to ways of improving both the business and his own leadership of it. He is always seeking to learn and grow and, like Andy, there is a purpose to his drive; in Stephen's case, it's his passion for great literature. Will all of this guarantee success? Maybe not. After a few years of working with him, it dawned on me that the consultancy I led had become much bigger than his business – our rate of growth had far exceeded his. Given the industry he was in, however, I could only marvel at his ability to grow the business at all, let alone becoming seen as the most progressive in the industry. He is still a role model for me.

Conclusion

We use hindsight to pigeonhole leaders as either heroes or villains, and then think that by copying one and avoiding the other, we can be heroes too, but it isn't as simple as that. Hindsight makes us seem wise, but it is much more difficult to see into the future and predict which of the current star CEOs will keep succeeding and which will eventually fail. By all means, learn from great leaders like Andy and Stephen. By all means, try to copy some of the things they do so well. Equally, look to the failures of others and try to avoid the same pitfalls, but don't do so in a simplistic way, assuming that everything about those who succeeded is good and everything about those who fail is bad. Discover the compelling person within you and judge others by more than how successful they seem to be this month.

References

Catmull, Ed (2014) *Creativity, Inc.: Overcoming the Unseen Forces that Stand in the Way of True Innovation*

Gino, F. (2013) *Sidetracked: Why Decisions Get Derailed, And How We Can Stick To The Plan*

Goldsmith, Marshall (2008) *What Got You Here Won't Get You There*

Malkiel, Burton, G. (2012) *A Random Walk Down Wall Street*

McClean, Bethany and Elkind, Peter (2004) *The Smartest Guys In The Room: The Amazing Rise And Scandalous Fall Of Enron*

Schmidt, F. L. and Hunter, J. E. (1998) *The validity and utility of selection methods in personal psychology: practical and theoretical implications of 85 years of research findings, Psychological Bulletin, 124*, 262-274

Segall, Ken (2013) *Insanely Simple: The Obsession That Drives Apple's Success*

Smith, Ed (2013) *Luck: A Fresh Look At Fortune*

Wai, Jonathan (2014) *Investigating The World's Rich And Powerful: Education, Cognitive Ability And Sex Differences, Intelligence, 46*, 54-72

Chapter 4

It's Just Maths:
How Statistics Can Explain Why Good Companies Get Worse

*"Take nothing on its looks; take everything on evidence.
There's no better rule."*
Charles Dickens, *Great Expectations*

Lies, Damned Lies, And Statistics

Nobody likes to think of themselves as a mug that listens to charlatans, so many of us are now prone to ask, "Where is the evidence?" We recognise that it is important not to take on trust the declarations and opinions of any old self-proclaimed expert, but rather they need to prove that what they have said is true. As I go about my job as a business psychologist and human resources professional, my clients will often ask me to back up my claims with some numbers. Even the casual reader of a business book will seek some kind of evidence that the solution they are being sold has some quantitative merit.

Well, ask and you shall receive. Every expert now comes fully-armed with the data and validation to prove that they have got a robust answer. The problem seems to be that we don't always fully understand the maths behind the claims that are being made (and sometimes nor do the people who are making them).

This chapter will give you an insight into some of the statistical concepts behind errors that are made by gurus of all types. I will assume minimal statistical knowledge, so apologies to those of you who are already experts – feel free to skip this chapter.

Lack of statistical training is not the only problem we will cover here, however, we also need to consider the intent with which the maths is deployed. In the main, people use statistics to make a point that they wish to make. They are highly motivated to dismiss unhelpful data, or manipulate things in their favour to make this point. Some of the very first experiments in the world of business and leadership fell prey to such issues. Take what is perhaps one of the most famous discoveries of modern management, The Hawthorne Effect. It is normally summarised in a pretty similar way. Here is the version in Peters and Waterman's *In Search of Excellence*:

"On the shop floors of Western Electric's Hawthorne plant, (Mayo) tried to demonstrate that better workplace hygiene would have a direct and positive effect on worker productivity, so he turned up the lights. Productivity went up as predicted. Then, as he prepared to turn his attention to another factor, he routinely turned the lights back down. Productivity went up again! For us, the very important message of the research that these actions spawned is that it is attention to employees, not work conditions per se, that has the dominant impact on productivity."

This is almost word for word the way that I was taught it in Psychology 101. What an amazing discovery it seemed, and so resonant with progressive thinking. Here were scientists playing with light levels, noise and other environmental factors, but what they discovered was that the best way to motivate people was to take an interest in them and maybe show you care. Lovely story, eh? And one that I myself have told many times over. Unfortunately, it wasn't quite that straightforward. It turns out that a whole bunch of other things were changing at the same time. Big things too, like the amount being paid for each unit of work, like the most troublesome workers being removed and the fastest workers being drafted in. However, that couldn't make for the neat and heart-warming story that we want to hear. It doesn't necessarily gel with the message your guru wants to tell, so the messy truth is ignored and the neat life lesson is kept.

In *The Management Myth: Debunking Modern Business Philosophy*, Matthew Stewart tracks down a review of the history of the experiment in which two of the Hawthorne experimenters, Homer Hilbarger and Donald Chipman, have a discussion about how the Hawthorne experiments were actually conducted. What they have to say confirms your worst fears about the manipulation of data:

Hilbarger: Well we know that we could take either side of any question and prove or disprove it in whatever way we want.

Chipman: Yes, they say that figures don't lie, but we have shown that we can take a set of figures and prove anything we want to.

Keeping awareness of this sad fact of deliberate manipulation at the back of our minds, I will now go through some of the most common areas that are misunderstood and can therefore be used to tell a story that isn't all that it seems. The areas I will look at are:

   a. Regression to the mean
   b. False correlations
   c. The Halo Effect
   d. Statistical significance

Regression To The Mean

Imagine that you are conducting an experiment into the effects of praise or criticism on the ability of children in a class. You create a task that involves showing the children a large number of dots on a piece of card and asking them to quickly estimate the number of dots. Those children who make close estimates are praised for their effort and those that guess poorly are criticised. If you conducted this experiment, what might you conclude if the children who were praised got worse in estimates in later tests, and the children who got criticised got better in their estimates? On first glance, a reasonable conclusion might be that the praise somehow diminished performance and you might generate a theory as to why. Perhaps, you might think, praise causes the children to rest on their laurels and try less hard next time. Perhaps criticism actually is good for children; it may steel their resolve and give them valuable feedback. While this may appear to be the conclusion that you should arrive at, in fact, you have been fooled by the phenomenon of regression to the mean.

The phenomenon comes from the observation that any data point that is away from the average score is likely to be closer to average next time. Why? Because it is easier to be less extreme than an already extreme finding than it is to be more. Think of someone making a world record javelin throw. What is more likely for their next throw – another new world record or a throw closer to the length they normally achieve? Clearly, it is the latter. However, if we didn't realise that simple statistical fact and made some kind of intervention with the thrower after the record (changing their run-up or grip), one might wrongly conclude that the change had somehow caused the poorer performance, when it really had nothing to do with it. Similarly, if that same thrower had fouled, the likelihood is that they wouldn't foul again next time. But if you were blind to that statistical truth and had made some intervention with the thrower (maybe a motivational pep talk), you might wrongly conclude that your intervention had done some good, when really it was irrelevant.

A very similar situation was first observed by Daniel Kahneman, who had worked with flying coaches in the Israeli air force. These coaches felt that when they praised people for good landings, they got worse, but when they shouted at them for making bad landings, they got better. The conclusion they came to was that praise softens you up, so only criticise. Kahneman, however, realised that what they were actually seeing was regression to the mean. Leonard Mlodinow describes it thus:

> "If a pilot made an exceptionally good landing – one far above his normal level of performance – then the odds would be good that he would perform closer to his norm – that is, worse – the next day. And if the instructor had praised him, it would appear that the praise had done him no good. But if the pilot made an exceptionally bad landing... then the odds would be good that the next day he would perform closer to his norm – that is, better. And if the instructor had the habit of screaming 'You clumsy ape' when a student performed poorly, it would appear that his criticism did some good. In this way, an apparent pattern would emerge: students perform well, praise no good; student performs poorly, instructor compares student to lower primate at high volume, student improves. The instructors in Kahneman's class had concluded from such experiences that their screaming was a powerful educational tool. In reality, it made no difference at all."

Take another example. If you have two parents who are both 6' 6", what do you think will be the likely height of their children – more or less than 6' 6"? It is tempting to feel that the child would be taller than the parents; that their height will in some way double up for their kids. True enough, the children would be likely to be taller than average, but they would actually be unlikely to be taller than their parents. Very few people are, and some of that statistical probability impacts upon these children too. If you look at the full picture, they are most likely to be shorter than their parents and closer to the mean.

This phenomenon is found pretty much everywhere. For example, Pankaj Ghemawat (1991) examined the return on investment (ROI) of a sample of 692 American companies over a 10-year period from the start of 1971. He looked at a group of top performers with an average ROI of 39% and a group of low performers with an average ROI of 3%. He then tracked the performance of both groups over time and found that both groups converged with the top performers, falling from 39% to 21%, and underperformers rising from 3% to 18%. They had regressed to the mean.

So the problem with regression to the mean is not that it happens. The problem is that we may forget that it is bound to happen and come up with false explanations of why the good got worse and the bad got better. Perhaps this explains why many of the highly-praised companies mentioned in the introduction to this book had got worse. Maybe the gurus were entirely correct in what they observed in these successful companies, and maybe the good habits that they described in their books are really worth following. The subsequent decline of these businesses therefore wasn't due to gurus picking badly, but the simple fact that, in general, over-performers regress to the mean. When you are Number One, there is zero probability of you getting better and a very high probability of getting worse. Such is the power of regression to the mean that it can swamp out the effect of a whole range of interventions, making it very hard for us to know what is and isn't working.

A final thought on this subject is that we should be wary of the turnaround story. A failing business drafts in a new CEO and things get better. The CEO reflects on what they did to achieve this miracle. The evidence sounds compelling; with the change of one key person at the top, the fortunes of the business changed too. No wonder these people get paid so much money. Maybe, but maybe not. Maybe the new CEO was the equivalent of the air force coach yelling 'You clumsy ape' and the improvement would have happened anyway. The challenge for everyone in this field is telling real, powerful interventions from sheer dumb luck.

Correlations Errors

When it comes to finding a link between some kind of leadership intervention and the success of a business, the first thing most people do is look for a correlation. Correlation is a way of measuring how much two separate sets of data vary together. In other words, as one increases, does the other also increase? If they match perfectly, their correlation is 1; if there is no relationship between the two, it is 0. It is drummed into every first-year statistics student that correlation does not mean causality. In other words, just because two things vary together, it doesn't mean to say that one of them is causing the other. Yet, time and again, that is exactly the implication that is being made by business writers of all types. On one level, you can't blame them; it is actually a very difficult thing to prove causality.

In the "hard sciences", the job is much simpler, as you can exactly control the inputs to a science experiment so that you only change one thing at a time and then measure the result. Social sciences like psychology are harder. For example, how do you know if parenting is more important than schooling when it comes to crime? Well, there are long and complex ways that you can tell, but you need to study many students over long time periods. You may even draw on identical twins that have been raised apart to rule out issues like genetics. Business science is harder still. Our ability to tweak just one variable in a business to check its effect is zero. We can't take two identical companies and try different approaches with each of them, so it is really tempting to look for correlations between what the businesses did and the results they got and then infer causality from any correlations we find. Unfortunately, there are a number of ways in which this can lead us to get things wrong. We can get it **the wrong way round**, we can miss a **hidden causal variable**, or the correlation may be a **random accident.** Let's look at each of these in turn.

Getting Causality The Wrong Way Round

When you see two things varying together, how do you know which one is causing which? Imagine for a moment that you are an alien, landing on the Earth for the first time. You see large moving objects in a clearing and decide that this is a good place to land. Your maps tell you that you have landed in the middle of something called "a wind farm". As you observe the movement around you, your sensors note a high correlation between the speed that the massive turbines are going at and the speed of the wind. There can only be one conclusion – these massive turbines are fans that have been installed to create wind and cool down the planet – that must be why they call it a wind farm.

Ludicrous, I know, but an all too easy mistake to make. I once worked for a business that noted that the more a company spent on our consulting, the higher the profits of that business. Our first reaction was to dance a celebratory jig and delight in the fact that we could demonstrate that increasing spending with us was good for your profits. Well that *may* have been true, but it is equally likely that highly profitable companies can afford to spend more on our type of consultancy, so it was their profitability leading to our consultancy rather than the other way round. Fortunately, we didn't over-claim credit, as we were first tempted to, but many businesses, fads or theories do.

Hidden Causal Variables

Did you know?

- Sleeping in your clothes is correlated with having a headache at work the next day.
- Ice cream consumption is correlated with shark attacks

Now one might claim that there is something about pyjamas that prevents headaches. One might suggest that sharks get driven into feeding frenzies, not because of the smell of blood, but rather the whiff of tutti-frutti. Or more plausibly, it might be that a third thing is causing both of the two that are correlated – drunkenness and hot days.

Once again, it is easy to spot the flaw in my silly example, but we can easily be blinded to it in other areas. If I could produce a study demonstrating a correlation between charitable giving and customer satisfaction, might you buy my thesis that customers value social responsibility so much that it improves their overall satisfaction? It may do, I may be right, but unfortunately, my correlation does not in any way prove it. The correlation may simply show that enlightened leaders often attend to both community and customer, and so when they take the helm of a business, both of those indicators increase at the same time.

Random Accident Correlations

If you put enough variables in a spreadsheet for long enough, sheer random chance will lead to totally unrelated variables ending up having a high correlation. A great example of one of these is given by Burton Malkiel in *A Random Walk Down Wall Street*. It is called the Super Bowl indicator. It seems that it is possible to link the winner of this game between NFL and AFL teams and the tendency for the market to wither, rise and fall. The claim is that an NFL win makes the market bullish, while an AFL victory makes markets fall. It isn't always right, but it seems to do better than pure chance. Even though, the only realistic explanation is that it is once again our human ability to link two things that are, in reality, independent.

The Halo Effect

One final correlational problem worth another mention is The Halo Effect. You will recall that this relates to our tendency to attribute positive characteristics that we have not observed to people who have another positive characteristic that we have seen. A positive glow appears to surround these people and so we wrongly credit them with more skills than they may possess.

A great example of this is given in Phil Rosenzweig's *The Halo Effect*. If you want to know more about this area, I heartily recommend it. He reports that, in 2001, after 9/11, George W. Bush's overall approval rating rose sharply as the nation united behind its leader. You can understand why this would happen, but more surprisingly, the number of Americans who approved of his handling of the economy also rose from 47% to 60%. In short, Americans were just thinking of Bush as "better", so they begin to rate him as better at everything, even things that he has not changed at all.

The problem with The Halo Effect is that many correlational studies inadvertently get confounded by this effect. One might, for example, try to use 360-degree feedback data as a source of insight into leadership. 360-degree feedback, if you are not already familiar with it, is a way of eliciting feedback from your boss, peers and direct reports. Frequently, you will find lots of rating scales that allow respondents to rate you on everything, from project management skills to your level of empathy. In such a study, you may well find that people who rate high on "listening" also rate high on "credibility", and so it would be easy to conclude that good listeners are more credible. Even without claiming that one causes the other, you may still be mistaken because of The Halo Effect. You might simply be observing that people who think that someone is good at one thing tend to think that they are good at everything.

Some years ago, I established an online 360-business that still runs today, and I took an interest in what was going on with the ratings. To help me understand more, I had something called a Factor Analysis done on various data sets. This method looks at correlations between variables and determines whether there are any underlying constructs that bind them together. Over and over again, I found the same constructs appearing and I ended up calling them "nice" and "competent". In essence, the raters were only telling us two things about the person they were rating: "Do I like them?" and "Are they good at their job?" If I like them, I tend to give all the people-focussed questions a high score, and if I think they are competent, I give all the task-focussed questions a high score.

Be warned – asking lots of questions of the same group of people can give an illusion of correlation when none exists.

Statistical Significance

The use of the term "statistical significance" seems to cause huge confusion for people because it is so hard to get the conventional meaning of the word "significant" out of one's head. In everyday life, a significant thing is something that is important and of consequence. So let's be 100% clear; saying that something is statistically significant does not in any way, shape or form mean that it is important. The next mistake that people make is to assume that if a finding is statistically significant, it must mean that it is a big result. The size of the difference must be large. Again, let's be clear – statistically significant differences don't need to be big (and frequently aren't). All statistical significance tells you is the likelihood of getting the result you did by chance; be that a big effect or a small one, an important finding or a trivial one.

Why do we need to look at statistical significance at all? Well let's go back to the basic problem of social sciences, the difficulty we have in proving anything. Imagine that you are holding a hammer at shoulder-height and let it drop to the ground, while filming yourself on a high-speed camera. By analysing the video, you should be able to accurately measure the effect of gravity. And guess what? If you did it again, you would get the same result. And again. And again. If only researching business success was so straightforward. Researching what makes a company successful is like having the same hammer occasionally drop to the ground, but at other times, it floats in the air. Sometimes its spins round your head and, very occasionally, it turns into a butterfly and flies away. Gravity may still be there, but it is really hard to measure.

Imagine now that you came across an extended family of 50 people and wanted to see if the males were, on average, taller than the females in this family. Well, you could measure them all and see. If the average of the males was higher than the average of the females, you will have found an undeniable fact because you had covered the whole population that you were interested in. What about if you just measure one of the males at random and one of the females at random? What if you found that the male was taller than the female? On this data point alone, could you say that the males were taller than the females? Probably not, especially if the female actually turned out to be a three-year-old girl. You simply haven't sampled enough of the population to know. In the terminology of statistics, we call the total number of people you are interested in **the population** and give it the symbol **N** (in this case, 50), and we call the total number that you measured the **sample**, and give it the symbol **n** (in this case, 2). The ratio of sample size to population size is clearly important in knowing whether the finding is indicative of a real difference. Now the problem that we have in understanding business is that we want to understand what works for all business, so **N** is in the millions. We can't measure all of them, so we take a sample and use statistics to tell us whether the finding we had was by chance. The closer **n** can be to **N**, the better.

Let's say we have a sample of five men in the family and they each measure 5'10", 5'10 , 5'11" 6'0" and 6'0". They are tightly clustered around an average height of 5'11". This tight clustering can give us some confidence in the typical male height. Whereas, if their heights were 5'0", 5.5", 5'11, 6'5 and 6'10", the average would be the same, but we would have much less of a sense of what was typical. This spread (covered by the statistical concept of standard deviation) must also be taken into account when deciding if any measured effect is real.

Finally, we need to look at the size of the difference itself. If you have measured nearly the whole population and the spread of scores is small, then even a tiny difference between men and women could be considered statistically significant. However, if you have only sampled a few people and those people show a big spread in scores, then you will need to see a whopping difference between your sample of men and women to have a statistically significant finding. Statisticians put all these factors into equations that tell them the likelihood that any particular finding is probable to have happened by chance. If they calculate that you would have got your findings by a chance of less than 1 in 20 times, they tend to say that you have a statistically significant finding.

This is all good stuff and the basis of social sciences. Just because our hammers suddenly turn into butterflies, it doesn't stop us using maths to find real effects. As you might have guessed, however, I have a few problems with where it can sometimes lead us.

Problem I: True But Dull

There are lots of disciplined and effective social scientists and business students out there who go to great lengths to gather as much data as possible and unearth *statistically* significant predictors of business success, but does that make them "significant" enough in the conventional sense of the word? You may well be able to prove beyond reasonable doubt that the right kind of investment in the right type of technology over a sustained period of time had a statistically significant 0.1% impact on business profits. But even if you did, would anyone be interested? Probably a few who have an interest in that technology, but it is hardly enough to build a business guru blockbuster around. And yet, that is exactly the type of finding that one is likely to get if playing strictly by the rules. Most business progress requires lots of effort for a long time for a small impact. Isn't it much more appealing to read a business book that says, "Do these five simple things and see your business skyrocket"? Of course it is, and so that is just the type of book that people want to both produce and read. If you want to read some true management science, I am sure that it is out there, but it is likely to suggest a hard and complex solution that will get you a small, incremental benefit. It is unlikely to show that taking one simple action will transform your business. Increasingly, it seems to me that you can read about *significant* effects (those that are big and important) or you can read about *statistically significant* findings (ones that are likely to be true), but it seems really hard to find ones that are both.

Problem 2: Unlikely Things Are Likely To Happen

So statistical significance is a great way to see if the results you are reporting could have happened by chance. Convention has it that you should only report findings that happen less than 1 in 20 times by chance.

But guess what? On average, that will happen 1 in every 20 times you look. This wouldn't be so bad if you got to hear about everything that every researcher looked at, but you don't. You never get to see all the things that they looked at and tried but were not statistically significant. They only write up the ones that were. So how do you know that the researcher didn't wade through random data countless times and then reported things that looked statistically significant but were actually just noise? This isn't a theoretical problem that I am reporting. It happens all the time. A business psychologist might look at hundreds of psychometric scores of CEOs and find the ones in which the successful CEOs score higher than the unsuccessful ones, and then develop a theory around the importance of these particular measures. The truth is that, if you do look at hundreds of measures, by sheer chance, several of them will look significant. Unless these studies are replicated enough times (as discussed in Chapter 1), they may well be worthless, but who is going to wait around for that when instead they can launch to the world their newfound success formula.

Problem 3: Researchers Cheat

As we saw in Chapter 2, there is some clear evidence that researchers nudge findings towards that magic 1 in 20 rule. The simple fact is that you will never be published, read and applauded unless you report some finding or other, so the temptation to cheat is huge. In general, we don't hear about this cheating, although there have been some notable exceptions. I have previously mentioned a couple of examples. The real problem is that, most of the time, we have no idea who is doing the massaging.

Problem 4: There Is Still Lots Of Overlap

Let's go back to the male-female height example. It is demonstrably the case that, on average, men are taller than women. So if, given no other information than name, you were asked, "Who would you like to help you reach the top shelf, John or Jane?", the most appropriate answer in the long-run is John. But just think for a moment about how many times that would be the wrong answer. While women are, on average, around four inches shorter than men, over a third of women are taller than the average male height of 5'9". You see, even when you have found a statistically significant difference, the gap may be small, and the spread of scores (standard deviation) may be broad.

Let me give just one more gender-based example of this effect. I am using these gender examples as they are easy for everyone to relate to and understand, not because I regard it as a particularly important area of misunderstanding. My aim is to show you how any statistically significant difference in business behaviour that your favourite guru quotes might not be as useful as you think. I am indebted to the *Sugar and Slugs* blog for this final example, which concerns what is known as the 2D:4D ratio. You may be familiar with this idea, and I looked at my own fingers when I first came across it. The idea is that the ratio of the length of your second digit (forefinger) and fourth digit (ring finger) is an indicator of gender:

"It seems to say, then, that we can set a threshold of one for the ratio, with men on one side and women on the other. If you have a ratio of less than one (longer ring finger), you have 'boy fingers', and if you have a ratio of greater than one (longer index finger), you have 'girl fingers'.

"Bet you just looked! Well those who look into these things do indeed find that there is a statistically significant difference between men and women on the 2D:4D ration. However, when you look at the overall distribution, you see that the overlap makes this finding almost useless.

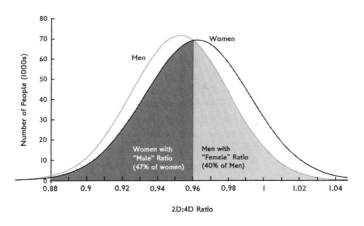

2D:4D Ratio

"As you can see, there is a lot of overlap. If we used finger length as a sex test, it would be right only 56.7% of the time. It's only better than 75% accurate for people with finger length ratios of 1.02 and above, and only 1.6% of the population fall into that category. It's only 90% accurate for people with a finger ratio of 1.06, which is a tiny 0.026% of the population.

"Also, while the test can accurately identify a very small number of women, it can never accurately identify men. It is at its most clear-cut at a ratio of 0.89; 3 out 5 people with that ratio (60%) are men.

"So while the researchers for this paper did find an actual 'statistically significant' difference between the finger ratios of men and women, in practice' the difference is not one we can usefully apply to individuals."

Back in the world of business, you will find exactly the same kind of overlap on a whole host of measures, but it is so easy to read that Management Style A produces statistically significantly better outcomes than Management Style B, and in our heads, make the false leap that Style A is *significantly* better than Style B in the everyday sense of the word.

If we believe that the findings reported in business books and articles contain some absolute truth along the lines that lead is heavier than air so hammers always fall, we may be kidding ourselves. Whatever you may read about companies with one characteristic being better than others that lack it, remember that the difference may be tiny and the overlap so great that a single bet on which company to back may be right only 51 times in 100.

Be As Rigorous As A Parapsychologist

While I was completing my PhD in the late 80s, like many others, I took the opportunity to earn some extra money by taking classes of undergraduate psychology students. The class that I was asked to teach was called critical analysis, and each week, a different speaker would select an academic paper for the students to critique. The idea was to teach the critical skills necessary for reading such papers. To my first class, I took along a paper that I was reading that was relevant to my PhD, but within which I saw a flaw. Sure enough, with a little guidance, the students saw that flaw, but I was impressed at how many other statistical and methodological problems they picked up on that I had missed. My teaching got good feedback, so I was asked to do another at somewhat short notice. Lacking adequate preparation time, I plumped for the article that happened to be top of the pile on my desk and, sure enough, the students tore that one apart too. Over the three years of my PhD, I realised that I could pick pretty much any article at random and attentive students could find fault with it. The amazing thing was that every one of those papers was accepted in distinguished journals and would be quoted for years to come in other papers as established fact.

Oddly enough, one of the few truly rigorous areas that I have encountered is the study of parapsychology. As most scientists are sceptics, anyone seeking to prove the existence of telekinesis, telepathy or whatever will have their work instantly eviscerated with the same passion as my undergraduates would show in class. As far as I can tell, the sceptics are winning as every attempt at proof fails to meet the required burden of proof. I now strongly believe that if we challenged business papers with the same fervour that was applied to parapsychology, none of those papers would make it either.

This chapter has been about why our attempts to get the scientific proof we need from the business gurus we read is fraught with difficulty, but despite the pessimism that may seem to be behind this train, I thought, I am hesitant to dismiss it as a result. Sure, correlation is often mistaken for causality and statistical significance may not coincide with conventional significance, but that doesn't mean that all the hours of research are wasted. The lesson we might take out of this is to be sceptical of bold claims of big effects on your business, but don't assume that they are entirely without foundation either.

Conclusion

So what do we make of all these mathematical issues? What can we glean from the numbers? It seems to me that a little knowledge is a dangerous thing, and so a limited knowledge of statistics can make us leap to unrealistic conclusions. Unfortunately, having a detailed knowledge is potentially much less interesting. It requires much more rigorous testing and validation. It requires people to replicate past findings, then be honest about the true size of any effect that is discovered and often, that doesn't make for bestsellers. Most importantly, it probably requires us to keep revisiting old truths and making minor adjustments to them, rather than being able to make a brand new, earth-shattering discovery. Perhaps it is our love of the new, the power of the next big thing that causes us to demand a new discovery. Our gurus respond to this need by giving us something new and, to make it credible, they must give us numbers to back it up, even if those numbers don't add up to much. Perhaps the root cause of this issue is our hunger for the next big things, so let us explore the world of management fads and fashions in the next chapter.

References

Ghemawat, Pankaj (1991) *Commitment: The Dynamics of Strategy*

Malkiel, Burton G. (2012) *A Random Walk Down Wall Street*

Mlododinov, Leonard (2008) *The Drunkard's Walk*

Peters, Tom and Waterman, Robert (1982) *In Search of Excellence: Lessons from America's Best-Run Companies*

Rosenzweig, Phil (2007) *The Halo Effect And Eight Other Business Delusions That Deceive Managers*

Stewart, M (2009) *The Management Myth: Why the Experts Keep Getting it Wrong*

https://sugarandslugs.wordpress.com/2011/02/13/sex-differences/

Chapter 5
Dedicated Followers Of Fashion:
Why We All Want The Next Big Thing

"Fashion is a form of ugliness so intolerable that we have to alter it every six months."
Oscar Wilde

Feeling Out Of Date?

Back in the early 90s, I worked as a trainer at a management institute, and one of the first courses that I was required to work on was called Leading Effective Teams. The institute itself was on a wonderfully calm and peaceful campus some miles outside of London. I was thrilled to be working in such a tranquil environment, helping to train the leaders of the future. While I was new to the programme, I had the benefit of working alongside a much more experienced trainer. The programme ran for a full four days and attracted managers from a range of different businesses. The institute had a good reputation and was generally regarded as being quite progressive. Participants would sit in a circle, much like a therapy group; there were no slides to show, but there were a number of handouts, containing interesting ideas and concepts that we would discuss in between running role-plays and doing exercises.

Day one of my first programme seemed to be progressing quite well until we got to the end of the afternoon and my colleague checked in with everyone to see how things were going. To my surprise, one of the participants was extremely unhappy. "My company has paid a lot of money for me to come here," he said, "yet these handouts that you have given contain references that go all the way back to the 1960s. Why aren't you teaching us something newer? I expect a place like this to only give us the latest thinking." While I froze like a rabbit in headlights, my colleague was more sanguine and asked the participant to bear with us until day two and wait to see what we would look at then.

The next day came and I was as interested to see what my colleague would come up with as the participants were. With a tremendous flourish, he took out and passed around a series of quotes and articles that he had sourced overnight. Every single one of them was more than a thousand years old, yet they fundamentally said exactly the same things that we had been discussing on day one. "What we have been discussing has been true for thousands of years," he said. "I don't think the last two decades has added much more to the debate." Gobsmacked at his audacity, the group just let him move on.

The memory of this event suddenly came back to me five years ago when I went to see a client of the executive assessment business that I was working for. Our business specialised in deep psychological interviewing of candidates for senior positions to help our clients make more informed hiring decisions. We were very good at what we did and had a methodology that had been refined, improved and tested over a number of years. Our client had called us in because she wanted to "refresh" what we were doing. She started to ask us what the latest big thing was. Trying to understand the reason for her question, we quizzed her about our existing work. Was something wrong or lacking? Had we made some bad calls? Was there any feedback that we needed to hear? She told us that everything was fine but we were still doing the same thing as last year, so she wanted to know what was new. In fact, there had been a few small changes in the year, as we had fine-tuned some details of the approach based on what we had learned about them as a client. We proceeded to list these small enhancements. "But it is basically still the same approach," she said. "I want something new." We offered up to her the most enhanced version of our approach; by investing an extra couple of hours with each person, we might make a small, incremental improvement to the output, but she made it clear that this wasn't really what she wanted. The conversation went round in circles for quite some time until we finally got the message; she didn't want the best method, she didn't even want a better method, she just wanted a newer one.

This chapter will look at this desire for newness – when is it helpful and when not. And how has this desire fuelled our gurus to provide us with fad after fad? Rather than dismiss it, however, let us strive to find the overlap between novelty and improvement, so that we might discard the rest.

What Makes A Fad A Fad?

Back in 2001, three researchers in Montreal, Danny Miller, John Hartwick and Isabelle Le Breton-Miller, did an interesting analysis of management fads since 1985. Their first task was to figure out what constituted a fad. They hit on the idea of searching academic databases for keywords in articles, and found that while some concepts appeared to have permanently entered the lexicon (e.g. globalisation), others had a brief surge in popularity and then faded away (e.g. TQM). They then chose to regard those that come and go as "fads" and those that stayed as "classics". While, by their own admission, this might not have been the most sophisticated approach, it did identify a number of potential fads that are worth looking at.

Now there may well be a range of reasons that citations of certain keywords rise and fall – the concept might change its name over time, the theory might be built on by something better – so it is worth looking at the content of these articles and not just their number. When they did so, Miller and his team found a common pattern. The early articles are when the fad is in the ascendancy. They declare that something new and revolutionary is here, that the old way must be discarded and the new way embraced; papers with titles like "*Total Quality: Wave of the Future*" and "*From Total Chaos to Total Quality*". After this initial call to arms, the next articles will tell you how to implement this great, new practice yourself, and will tell you what a positive difference it seems to be making, so we get "*TQM: Understanding the Basics of Total Quality Management*" and "*Total Quality Management: Giving Companies a*

Way to Enhance Position in the Global Market". Now that your fad is part of the mainstream, the last luddites are encouraged to get on board with papers like this somewhat aggressive *"Industry to B Schools: Smarten Up on TQM or Else"*.

Initial questions may now be raised about your fad, but they are somewhat tentative and suggest the problem may be that some people are not doing it right. *"Warning: This Good Idea May Become a Fad"*, *"Managing for Quality: High Priests and Hucksters"*, *"Reengineering: Beyond the Buzzword"*. Unfortunately, this is just the beginning of the end. Soon, the real issues become apparent – *"Ten Reasons Why TQM doesn't work"*, *"The Hocus Pocus of Reengineering"* – and we are finally left scrambling around to see if anything is worth saving; *"TQM: More Than a Dying Fad?"* and *"Why TQM Fails and What to Do About It"*.

How Might You Spot A Fad?

The Miller et al analysis also gives us some clues that might help us to spot a fad in the making. By comparing the "fads" and the "classics", they were able to identify the common characteristics of those ideas that make a big, quick splash and then fade away.

1. **Simplicity** – what is striking about the faddish ideas is that they are very simple to grasp. We tend to have to worry about very few factors in order to make them work. The story is easy to share and the message is clear. If only the world was as simple as the solution being sold.

2. **They promise the world** – without fail, spectacular claims will be made about the upside of adopting the desired approach.

3. **Universality** – amazingly, the solution offered seems to work in every department of every company in every industry. You don't need to worry if this is the right solution for your precise context – apparently, it is right for every context.

4. **Easy to implement** – they tend to offer solutions that can be quickly rolled out and may involve simple attitude change rather than something costly or complex to bring in.

5. **In tune with zeitgeist** – fads are always of the moment, and address the fears and concerns of the day (e.g. Japanese approaches became popular as the US started to lose its lead in the world).

6. **Novel not radical** – despite their claims, fads tend not to be genuinely revolutionary; they tend to be the repackaging of something that already existed.

7. **Star quality** – they nearly always have a star individual or business as their standard-bearer. As discussed in earlier chapters, a high-performing company or CEO is often cited as the reason to adopt a certain approach.

8. **Entertainment value** – "Framed with labels and buzzwords, lists and acronyms, fads are often presented in a way that is articulate, memorable and upbeat."

Well, these insights were gained back in 2001. What about the current crop of leadership fashions? Two of the biggest panaceas of recent years are "Authentic Leadership" and "Mindfulness" – perhaps it is worth reflecting for a moment how many of the eight fad characteristics apply to them. Have a little read through... Yup, that's right. They all do.

Two Reasons For The New

Before we go too overboard in our condemnation of apparent fads, it is worth considering the other side of the argument. Might there be a legitimate reason why perfectly good ideas come and go quickly? Is it always a sign of a bad idea for it to be popular one year and abandoned the next? Maybe not. I can see at least two very good reasons why what appears to be a here-today-gone-tomorrow fad might be a good thing.

Firstly, the world is changing, markets are changing, and business demands are changing. It is quite conceivable that a new challenge might emerge, a management technique is adopted to handle it, and this technique becomes such a fundamental part of business that we cease to call it out. Take, for example, global team working. Some years ago, every one of my clients was wrestling with how to run good global team meetings and often struggled with clunky teleconferencing systems. We would spend a lot of time talking about the difference between face-to-face and teleconference meetings. While not completely cracked, this is a need that rarely gets mentioned now. The technology has improved and video calls on tablet computers are now the norm. People are probably now much more adept and relaxed than they used to be. New protocols and ways of working have been embedded. The need for intervention is now much less acute. So were a flurry of articles about global working 10 years ago a fad with no basis? Of course not, they had relevance then and so served a purpose.

Notwithstanding my example at the start of this chapter about my co-facilitator who came up with thousand-year-old articles, it is also possible that people have changed. I don't mean that the fundamentals of human nature have shifted, but perhaps the nature of people in the workplace has undergone some significant revolutions – not least the steps that are finally beginning to be made in relation to gender. Indeed, I recently wrote an article entitled *Which Decade Are You Leading In?*, pushing back on the continual requests to identify how Indian leadership differed from American, or Mexican from British. I decided to focus on the changing nature of the employee-employer relationship over time in various countries, an extract of which I will share with you here.

Perhaps we should obsess less about enduring cultural differences and increase our sensitivity to what is happening now in the lives of those we lead. The nature of leadership is ever-changing – not necessarily because of changes brought about by leaders, but because of the evolving power, values and needs of those they direct. Today's "followers" are nothing like those of yesteryear. As the novelist, L. P. Hartley, famously observed in The Go-Between: *"The past is a foreign country: they do things differently there."*

Over the centuries, there have been huge changes in the relationship between those in power and those who provide labour, deriving in no small part from increasing freedoms. The earliest models of slavery and indentured servitude saw those in power treat workers as their possessions; and, even when freedoms were subsequently won, business owners still wielded the great balance of power. Although the most extreme abuses of liberty were gone, child labour and other forms of exploitation remained rife, with both the law and economic power still firmly in the hands of the men who led.

Progressive reforms and the rise of organised labour unions led to great improvements to working life. But, for the best part of the 20th century, the financial disparity between rich and poor continued: you still needed your employer much more than they seemed to need you. The command and control style of management that I first encountered was the tail end of a period characterised by a high degree of compliance from workers, who were managed rather than led.

One of the great accelerators of the power shift in recent years has been the changing social contract within companies. The quid pro quo for the death of the "job for life" is the emergence of new, cross-organisational careers – opening up new choices. Organisations have consequently needed to pay much more attention to attracting and retaining talent, and the way people are led has changed accordingly. It turns out that those with real talent and choice don't like being directed. They know they can go out and find successful and fulfilling lives, indebted to no boss, hence the importance now placed on creating a meaningful and purposeful, values-oriented workplace to attract, inspire and motivate such talent.

When Followers Become Leaders

The way people have had to lead and manage others has changed extraordinarily. But the momentum hasn't been driven by the choices of leaders, or held back by national cultures. It has been determined by the new freedoms and powers of those they lead.

Good leadership is situational and must be defined as that set of behaviours that attracts followership in the here and now. That has big implications for the lens through which we assess the differences we encounter around the world. A particular leadership culture in any given country may well be contextual — and, as such, is likely to change.

Rather than asking what type of leadership style is best in Vietnam, Brazil or Norway, therefore, I would advise clients to explore more immediate and salient questions. What is happening now in that country, its economy and my industry? What are the hopes, dreams and aspirations of those individuals I lead?

How is followership changing – and, therefore, what leadership style might be needed in future?

This takes a good deal more effort: what is right today will be wrong tomorrow. But it is surely preferable to subscribing to the dangerously cosy notion that we can study some static model of a national leadership style and achieve instant success.

Perhaps the ever-changing nature of management trends reflects a degree of evolutionary progress. Perhaps instead of seeing them as temporary ripples on an unchanging business pond, we might consider new ideas and thinking as the babbling of a brook as it makes its way to the river. We could then celebrate the fact that the ideas of the past may not work in the future, and so new ones will always be needed.

The second reason that I question the validity of universal criticism of new "fads" is that they may be a necessary way of keeping old learning alive. It is always pleasing to dismiss an idea as old wine in new bottles, but is that always so wrong? Maybe the new bottles can bring an important and unchanging truth to a new audience. Each generation may need this wisdom to be wrapped in its own language and mythology in order to be really able to relate to it. Is that such a bad thing? In their article, which we explored above, Miller et al say:

"The motivational distinctions made today by human relations psychologists were well understood in ancient Rome by the philosopher, Marcus Aurelius, and historian, Titus Livius. Moreover, concern with efficiency and quality was very much in evidence in the writings of Adam Smith. Thus, the fad auteurs have taken old ideas and reformulated them to have greater appeal, perhaps by using simplification, memorable examples, and new vocabularies (satisfiers vs motivators; Theory X, Y and Z)."

To which I am inclined to say "good for you, *'fad auteurs'*"; most leaders don't read much Titus Livius these days, so at least you have brought this wisdom to their attention. Is it really fair to criticise something solely on the basis that it has been said before? If it was true then isn't it better to repeat an old truth than to invent a new lie? Furthermore, isn't it better to retell a great story so that someone else can hear it, rather than leave them in ignorance because the original is inaccessible?

This also takes us back to "Mindfulness", which we saw had all the hallmarks of a fad – one of which is that it appears to repackage in modern terminology age-old Buddhist practices. Well maybe that's its redeeming feature. The longevity of such practices suggests to me that generations have found value in them, so giving it a fancy, new name to bring it to the attention of a new audience may not be such a bad thing.

False Market Creation

Before you start thinking that I have become a convert to the gurus, time for another reality check. While there may be **good** reasons for changing management fashions, there are also a whole heap of **bad** ones. Remember the HR person at the start of this chapter who was demanding that I show her something new? Well, where there are buyers, there are bound to be sellers. If the market wants something new, we will give them something new (even if it is just repackaging something old). In addition to the pull from customers, there is also the push from sellers who want to stand out from their competition and create new needs that they can service. In his analysis of the strategy-consulting industry, Matthew Stewart tells this story.

> "The most general and far-reaching consequence of turning the discipline of strategy into a consulting product has been the creation of an artificial need for newness in the business – for fashions in strategy. In the 1980s, as it became clear that the matrix was losing its lustre, BCG announced that 'today, time is at the cutting edge'. The firm promptly began to tout time-based competition – the idea that, roughly speaking, the last one to market is a rotten egg – as a basis for all strategy worthy of its name. By the early 1990s, however, time had evidently run out on the time-based movement. Facing spirited, new competition from the 'core capabilities' crowd, BCG's strategy gurus rolled out a 'me too' product: 'capabilities-based competition'.

Later in the same decade, as the dot-com bubble loomed, the very same gurus declared that 'every business is an information business'."

This quote lays bare some of the fundamental issues of the consulting industry. To survive and beat your competitors, you cannot get left behind, and that means always inventing something new. A new catchphrase may be all you need, but the relentless draw is to the next big thing rather than really testing, refining and improving what you have done in the past. Of course, it may also be that what you last did for your client wasn't that great. Maybe it made you lots of money, but it didn't deliver the dreamed-of transformation, and so the last thing you want to do is hang around discussing it. Much better to pull something new out of the hat to capture everyone's attention. After all, it is much harder to hit a moving target.

Management Theories Aren't Gadgets

I love my gadgets. I don't exactly queue outside the Apple Store for every new release, but I am at the early adopter end of the spectrum. In my defence, it is not just that I am seduced by shiny things; it is also because many new releases bring new functionality, better battery life, or some other enhancement. In the world of gadgets, the new – by and large – is better than the old. As a result, it is easy for us to equate the words "newest" and "latest" with the "best". Of course, even in technology, this can be a mistake. Tech lovers will always tell you never to buy version 1.0 of a new product as it is still buggy, but in business, the link between newer and better is even more tenuous.

Knowing full well that we have a bias towards newer being better, any salesperson worth his or her salt will play up the new. I have lost count of the times that colleagues have said something along the lines of "What new thing have we got to say?" Why? Because if we don't have anything new to say, we don't have an excuse to reach out to customers. I can just imagine how far I would get if I was trying to awaken a dormant client with a line like, "Having good interview skills is still as important as it was 10 years ago; would you like to talk about ensuring your people are still fully trained?" I doubt I would get much more than a shrug. However, I might tempt someone with... "Our latest research shows the impact of the cutting-edge iView techniques; would you like to learn more?" If only because that person might feel exposed by not knowing what on earth iView was.

Is that all it takes to seem modern? A fancy, new name? It seems that to some people it is. At least, it may be enough to convince someone that you have something new and, by and large, the new stuff in our high-tech world is better than the old. The problem is that leadership theories aren't gadgets. It is harder to introduce a funky, new product that renders all predecessors obsolete. It takes time to learn and refine our approach to the engagement of people and the management of complex structures. We need time and patience to evolve our practice in a world that delights in revolution.

What Was It Like In The Olden Days, Daddy?

Through this chapter, we have looked at both the light and the shade of fads and fashions. They can genuinely build on past theories and, therefore, help slowly enhance the health, wealth and happiness of our society. In doing so, we might really be standing on the shoulders of giants. On the other hand, we might just be stepping on their toes. The fads may, at best, be repackaging old theories and, at worst, be cynical sales ploys to woo a novelty-hungry audience. The problem is: how do we know?

We might normally turn first to the statistics and evidence, but Chapter 4 highlighted many of the issues associated with that approach. We also need to engage our critical faculties and ask some important questions. For example, is there a clear rationale for why the old way was not working or was wrong? This sounds like a sensible course of action. If we can genuinely see that an old way doesn't work then that compels us to do something new, rather than embracing newness for the sake of it. If you look around, you will find that many of the gurus are claiming to do just that, but in doing so, they often use a very biased description of what the old approach was. You might well see a chart like this.

OLD MILLENNIUM LEADERSHIP	NEW MILLENNIUM LEADERSHIP
Administration	Innovation
Relies on Control	Inspires Trust
Asks How and When	Asks When and Why
Eye on Bottom Line	Eye on Horizon
Systems and Structure	People

On first glance, this looks reasonable enough, but actually, it is a convenient misremembering. Actually, those comparator pairs come from a famous **1985** article by Warren Bennis and Burt Nanus. It seems that we didn't think so differently back in the 1980s after all. These charts also appeal to our ego, as it is easy for us to see ourselves reflected in the right-hand, modern leadership style. That frisson of excitement about being one of the new-style managers helps us warm to the theory being expanded. It also helps the writer take something that is only marginally new and make it seem like the desired revolution.

Conclusion

Ultimately, when we try to decide whether to adopt a certain fad or listen to the latest guru, we all tend to find ourselves wrestling with the question – does it work? This sounds like exactly the right question. However, I believe that even this is the wrong question to ask, and comes from us all being trapped in a similar unhelpful mind-set. In the next chapter, I will explain why.

References

Ballman, P. (2015) What Decade Are You Leading In? *YQ9* available from www.ysc.com

Bennis, W. and Nanus, B. (1985) *Leadership: The Strategies For Taking Charge*

Malkiel, Burton G. (2012) *A Random Walk Down Wall Street*

Matthew, Stewart (2009) *The Management Myth: Why The Experts Keep Getting It Wrong*

Miller, D., Hartwick, J., Le Breton-Miller, I. ((7-16) July-August, 2004) *How To Detect A Management Fad – And Distinguish It From A Classic, Business Horizons, 47/4*

Chapter 6
Living In A Bubble:
Why Gurus Are Always A Part Of The Illusion Of The Day

"It is the obvious which is so difficult to see most of the time. People say 'It's as plain as the nose on your face.' But how much of the nose on your face can you see, unless someone holds a mirror up to you?"
Isaac Asimov – I, Robot

How Many Dimensions Can You See?

I was recently introduced to the story of *Flatland*. The hero is a triangle who moves around a two-dimensional world. One day, the hero is shown three-dimensional sphere and is able to comprehend the third dimension. The story then tells of his struggles to convince his fellow Flatworld people of the existence of that dimension, as he doesn't even have the words to describe it. Whether we admit it or not, we are all locked into some frame of reference that is so fundamental that we do not even perceive that it is there. The flat world people never questioned their two-dimensional assumptions, as they were so much part of their perceived reality that they didn't even realise they were only seeing part of the story. I guess the reason that this childhood book has stuck with me has been that I am always wondering what things are beyond the limit of my own perception; what assumptions I have made that make me blind to a broader truth. Perhaps it is the nature of such things that I will never be able to really know my deepest false perceptions, but there are two important assumptions that many of us make that I have increasingly come to believe are getting in the way of us seeing the real truth about leadership.

I am very aware that there will be many other assumptions that I have not noted or named that may be of equal importance, but this chapter will explore the two that are now clearest to me. The first is the belief in cause and effect and the second is the belief in the importance of success.

Cause And Effect

Physics was one of my favourite subjects at school. I enjoyed the order and predictability that it provided. It seemed to me that if I could understand a few immutable laws then everything else in the world could be figured out. Of course, when I say physics, I do obviously mean the physics of Newton. While the theories of relativity and quantum physics were known and established, in practice, 14-year-old boys need only concern themselves with gravity, momentum and the like. It made such perfect sense and could explain so many things with so much accuracy. In management bestseller, *Surfing the Edge of Chaos: The Laws of Nature and the New Laws of Business*, Richard Pascale describes it well:

"From the 1680s onward, Isaac Newton was the new Moses, presenting a few simple equations – the laws of nature – which never failed in predicting the tides, the orbit or movement of any object that could be seen or felt. Output was exactly proportional to input. Everything was equal to the sum of its parts. Newton's mechanics seemed so perfect, so universal, that they became the organizing principles of all post-feudal society, including armies, churches, and economic institutions of every kind... The very equations of economics, including many we use today, were built explicitly on the principles of mechanics and thermodynamics, right down to the terms and symbols. The economy was said to 'have momentum', was 'well oiled' or 'gaining steam'.

"As a model of everything, Newtonianism, it turned out, had limitations. It worked only within the narrow range of Newton's instruments. The laws of nature fell to pieces in space, as Einstein's relativity physics showed, and at the subatomic level, as quantum physics showed. Scientists realised that however useful in solving smooth, mechanical problems, Newton's calculus was meaningless in understanding the vast preponderance of nature: the motion of currents, the growth of plants, the rise and fall of civilisations.

"Einstein's insight into relativity – overturning, as it did, the orderly world of classical physics – extended broad influence over many other disciplines. Early in the twentieth century, relativism was mirrored in art (Picasso and Pollack), Poetry (T. S. Eliot), music (Stravinsky), literature (James Joyce), and interpretive religion. Object and observer became inseparable. Structure was connected to process, the medium to the message, doing to being. The rational and analytical were inseparable from the emotional and intuitive. Except in management."

Let me explain some more. Conventional Newtonian physics shapes so much of our understanding of the world. We know that if we act on an object, it will move unless it is opposed by some other force. This knowledge informs the way we live each and every day. The milk will stay in the fridge where I put it unless someone else takes it. When I put in more effort and energy at work, I seem to get more or better output. The world is a sensible and rational place. At the same time, we intellectually know that the universe is actually a more confusing place and there are places where our assumptions can be proved to be untrue, yet we still stick to our simple understanding of the world. Why? Because it works. I am unlikely to either go to space or spend time at the large hadron collider in CERN, so for all practical purposes, I need only attend to Newton.

So, what has any of this got to do with leadership? Well, much of our thinking and action in the workplace is based on a Newtonian style of thinking. Our approaches to objective setting, project management, accounting, input and output measures, and many other areas, all base themselves on simple rules of cause and effect, and you know what, it seems to work. At least, it seems to work on a small scale. When I am working as an individual contributor or with a small team, the simple view of cause and effect does very well. So perhaps this is the reason that management has largely ignored the relativist revolution embraced by the arts; it simply isn't needed. The problem is that the Newtonian rules do break down, not in space or at subatomic levels, but rather at the large-scale, organisational or total market level. When we enter the world of large "living" systems, things become much more complicated. We need to embrace the theories of chaos and complexity, but we are resistant to doing so.

It seems to me that through any leaders' early years in business, a certain set of rules and way of thinking works very well. In fact, they work so well that we all begin to rely on them and to believe that they are universal. We figure out that certain types of input lead to certain types of output. If you can just figure out how the machine works, you can easily be its master. When one reaches the heady heights of the C-Suite and applies the lessons learned earlier in our careers, it is therefore natural to try to figure out how this bigger machine works. I often have senior people talk to me about figuring out which levers to pulls. Often they do so with an increasing sense of panic as, for the first time in their careers, lever-pulling doesn't seem to be making a difference. In desperation, they will often turn to consultants or other gurus to get the answer. And each of these experts in turn will say, "Don't worry, I know the lever to pull. In fact, I will pull it for you if you pay me."

As long as they stick in the Newtonian mind-set, seeking the lever to pull, they may well be doomed, as they do not realise that they have crossed a threshold, which is the management equivalent of going into space or to subatomic levels. They are now in the realm of complex, adaptive systems, and the old rules of cause and effect no longer apply. There is now another dimension to be perceived and it requires abandoning all of the assumptions that have proved so useful earlier in a leader's career.

The Importance Of Agency

If reliance on a Newtonian view of the world wasn't enough, we also seem to have a deep psychological need for something known as "agency". In other words, we like to feel that our actions have impact and we can therefore make a difference to the world. An experiment highlighting this need for agency is described in *A Random Walk Down Wall Street*:

> "In one study, subjects were seated in front of a computer screen divided by a horizontal line, with a ball fluctuating randomly between two halves. The people were given a device to press to move the ball upward, but they were warned that random shocks would also influence the ball so that they did not have complete control. Subjects were then asked to play the game with the object of keeping the ball in the upper half for as long as possible. In one set of experiments, the device was not even attached, so the players had absolutely no control over the movements of the ball. Nevertheless, when subjects were questioned after a period of playing the game, they were convinced that they had a good

deal of control over the movement of the ball. (The only subjects not under such an illusion turned out to be those who had been clinically diagnosed with depression.)"

This example reminds me of the contortions that a tenpin bowler might go through when they have already thrown the ball, yet still twist their bodies in an apparent attempt to make the ball swing one way or another. We deeply wish to control things that are outside our control and may even convince ourselves that we are doing so. Perhaps the basis of all superstitions is the attempt to have agency in an uncertain and unpredictable world. This tendency is not limited to humans; the father of behaviourism, B. F. Skinner, even observed it in pigeons. He noted that in experiments that required pigeons to press levers to release food, the pigeons would also incorporate moves, twists and turns that had no effect on the lever, but had somehow been associated in the pigeons' mind with the release of food. Scott Adams, the creator of Dilbert, has seen similar behaviour in his dog:

"When my dog, Snickers, wants to play fetch in the backyard, she follows me around and stares into my eyes with freakish intensity, as if using her Jedi doggy powers on me. More often than not, it works. I know what she wants and take a break from work to accommodate her. The interesting thing is that I am not sure she understands that it is my choice whether I go play with her or not. Her mental control of me works so well that I'm certain she thinks all that matters is how hard she stares at me and how vividly she imagines herself chasing a tennis ball.

"To me, the fascinating thing about Snicker's flawed view of the world is that it works perfectly. She has a system for getting what she wants, and it *seems* to work, albeit for different reasons than she imagines. The deeper reality is that I've learned that her stares mean it's time for some tennis ball fun. My experience with Snickers begs a bigger question: Are humans so different from dogs in terms of having totally flawed assumptions about reality, and do our flawed assumptions work for reasons we don't understand?"

I wonder how many processes and practices in the typical workplace are based on false beliefs about causality. Do we have superstitions that lead us to methodically go through the same routine over and over without it having any real impact? Perhaps these things just give us the illusion of control that we crave. Pascale et al give a good example. Do the annual reward processes that we take employees through really add value, or are we like bowlers willing that ball to keep out of the gutter?

"Not long ago, *The Wall Street Journal* published a thoughtful critique of contemporary reward systems. Its main finding was that, despite the current popularity for pay-for-performance, balanced scorecards, and team-based rewards, most of the schemes fail to produce the overall broad outcome desired. Dogged pursuit of the perfect reward scheme, as Samuel Johnson might have said, represents the triumph of hope over experience."

From early in my career, I have seen and even taught flowcharts that supposedly demonstrate how cause and effect works when it comes to employee motivation. Way back in 1970, Victor Vroom taught us that if someone values the reward (valency), believes that they can do what is expected of them (expectancy), and actually believes that they will get the reward (instrumentality) then you will be able to manage that employee's behaviour. I actually think that this probably works on an individual basis, but it requires a sensitive enough manager to really understand what their people really value and what they are really capable of. The problem comes when you scale up this thinking to organisations of tens or hundreds of thousands of people. You then find yourself moving from a Newtonian world of cause and effect to a highly complex and chaotic living system, and the whole thing breaks down. As an individual leader, you may well think it should work for the organisation, because it works for you as an individual. You therefore roll out the practice that made you successful to your army of followers, and then struggle to figure out why this lever, when scaled up, doesn't seem to be working.

I Should Be So Lucky

Many people with a strong sense of agency will say things like, "You make your own luck." The idea that they are at the mercy of fortune is not tolerated. "Let's not leave anything to chance," they say. I suspect, but cannot prove, that people who operate in this manner actually do very well, as they act on their world rather than waiting to be a victim of it. Indeed, most of the time, it is my own personal orientation. The problem can be that we take this thinking so far that we believe we are such masters of our own destiny that luck doesn't even play a part. We end up wanting everything to operate like a tightly-controlled Newtonian mechanics experiment. What does a society end up looking like if we follow this line of thinking to its natural conclusion? Well, as luck would have it, back in the 1920s, the anthropologist, E. E. Evans-Pritchard, spent time with a Sudanese tribe called the Azande, who rejected the idea of luck. For them, all misfortune must have a human cause – someone to blame. They therefore developed a strong concept of witchcraft. If a person gets ill or a crop fails, you just need to figure out who is casting the spell against you. As you might imagine, this led to a society full of mistrust and suspicion. Ed Smith considers the modern-day version of this in *Luck*.

> "The Cambridge academic James Laidlaw used Evans-Pritchard's Azande study to explore whether Western society, too, is producing an unhelpful surfeit of what he called 'agency'. Are we, too, moving towards believing that everything is caused by deliberate human intervention? What happens when there is too much agency and not enough luck?
>
> "Laidlaw goes on to argue that our own society is undergoing its own kind of 'proliferation of

agency'. Television adverts ask you to consider taking legal action to gain 'compensation' for injuries that you'd not previously considered to have been anyone's fault. If you can find a causal link, however tenuous, between an ailment and your employer, you could benefit financially. In effect, the law firm is asking you to turn an accident into an act of 'agency' for which someone is directly responsible."

For several years, I have worked with a global organisation that is so mired in this agency and blame mind-set that almost paralyses it. Every mistake that is ever made is pursued with a vengeance until someone can be found to blame. Oddly, nothing too bad happens to this person, they tend not to get fired, but the shame and humiliation is great. The net result of this is a mass avoidance of decision-making. At least 10 people seem to be involved in any decision, so that everyone can claim that they didn't make a decision alone and therefore cannot be the person to blame.

An overdose of agency therefore has two negative effects; it causes a false sense of control over complex systems and it leads to an unhealthy blame culture. On the other hand, on the micro-scale, dealing with one issue at a time, a high sense of agency is almost essential for success. If we don't believe we can impact the world and make a difference, then we are likely to become passive victims and fall by the wayside. We therefore need to wrestle with a fundamental paradox in our minds.

The Agency Paradox

To me the starkest example of the need to believe in your own complete agency at the same time as accepting that you are fooling yourself is sports psychology. Most athletes in most sports are likely to do some form of positive visualisation prior to play. They will focus their mind and "see" themselves winning. This visualisation needs to be vivid and believable. Of course, if we take one-on-one sports, like fencing, both players will enter the salle with the same winning mind-set. If they are professional, both must believe they will win, but one of them will be wrong. Of course, if the loser really had believed that visualising winning makes you win, then they would abandon the method the first time that they lost. They would say to their coach, "I believed I could win and I didn't, so this *believe in yourself stuff* doesn't work." Maybe the athlete thinks to herself, "Well believing in yourself 100% doesn't make you 100% likely to win, but it does make you *more* likely to win than if you didn't believe it." Well this is probably false too, as I suspect all fencers visualise winning, but the number of winners has stayed doggedly at 50% for as long as people have fenced. The true thing that can be said, however, is, "Failing to visualise success is likely to lead to failure".

This construct probably extends to the many lessons put in the early guru books that so confused me. Customer centricity won't make you succeed, but lacking it may make you fail; employee engagement can't guarantee success, but losing it could spell disaster. Monitoring your competition can't ensure you will beat them, but ignoring them is a real risk. Tight budgetary control won't ensure profit, but reckless spending is sure to reduce it. It seems to me that all good businesses follow many of the lessons of the business writers, but the reason that so many then go on to fail is that these things influence success, but in no way guarantee it, in part because so many others are trying to do the same thing. I am sure that every fencing champion will tell you how well they practised, visualised success and played the inner game; unfortunately, so will the runners–up.

And so to back to agency in business. Somehow, a leader needs to have a strong sense of agency and believe in their ability to impact the world, and that *cause* will lead to *effect* in a predictable manner. However, they also need to know and understand that this is an illusion and, furthermore, it becomes a dangerous illusion when you apply it to an organisation of many thousands of people.

The Chaos And Complexity Of Large Systems

Around the same time that I heard Tom Peters speak for the first time, another set of books came on to the market that had a profound effect on me; they related to the ideas of chaos theory and complexity. I have two of these books sat in front of me as I write; James Gleick's *Chaos: Making a New Science*, and Kevin Kelly's *Out of Control: The New Biology of Machines, Social Systems, and the Economic World*. You may even recall from my introduction the name of the book that I tried to write as a young man, *The Chaotic Catalyst*. I believed then, and still believe now, that an understanding of chaotic systems and complex systems is a necessary part of understanding business. Once a system becomes complicated and has feedback loops built into it, it soon moves beyond our ability to make simple cause and effect connections. I am far from the first person to point this out and will not be the last. The likes of *Surfing the Edge of Chaos: The Laws of Nature and the New Laws of Business* have done a good job of applying the thinking in a business context.

These pages are insufficient to explain those theories in detail, so I recommend the above books that will introduce you to a whole new lexicon of fractals, strange attractors and deterministic, non-period flow. In essence, these theories look at what happens when we go from one cause and effect to many millions of them that are all interconnected and flow backwards as well as forwards; the complexity that one gets with the weather or the flow of the ocean. This complexity that ensues is not a wild beast, however, as there is order to be found in the self-organisation that results. We cannot predict and control how the patterns of a snowflake develop, but we can admire the beauty of the form when it does. Complex, adaptive systems are much more robust than an engineered or designed one; they may even have what Nassim Taleb calls "antifragility" – they get stronger when shaken, rather than weaker. Many thinkers agree that, while we may try to manage them like machines, organisations are actually more like these complex systems with each employee at a node, and yet we don't seem to be listening. The problem is that, while we know that these thinkers are right, we find it hard to apply their lessons. In some ways, it is similar to the fact that we know Newtonian physics has been superseded by relativity, yet we still live in a Newtonian world.

Once again, I think the problem comes back to the fact that our simple cause and effect thinking does work for a lot of the time, in a lot of situations, with a lot of people. My career has been built on my sense of control, mastery, logic and agency. The same is probably true for most leaders. It is therefore very hard for a leader to cross a threshold and say – I now lead a complex living system and that requires a whole new set of skills. The mind-set shift is like going from being a mechanic to being a gardener. I start from a position where I can exactly manage, polish and understand every moving part. If something breaks, I can find the root cause and fix it. Suddenly, I am in a new situation where I cannot control the timing of every flower that opens. I can influence it, I can create the right conditions, I can prune where needed and fertilise as required, but I cannot manage it in the same way as a car. Unsurprisingly, this is a difficult transition to make. Leaders desperately want to know which button to press to increase potato yield or flower life. They are tempted therefore to act like mechanics. "Let's dig it up, take it apart and see what is wrong." I realise that even this example has limitations. Modern gardeners know lots about how plants work and can manage them more than ever before. But an organisation consisting of thousands of free-willed people is far more complex than any garden I have ever known, yet it is still tempting to manage it like a machine, rather than embrace it as a living system.

Social Engineering

Of course, many leaders and writers do fully embrace that they are leading social systems and not controlling machines. However, they are normally reticent to go the whole hog and embrace chaos and complexity. Instead, I find them tending to settle at the half-=way house of social engineering. They accept that it is a social system, but still, at heart, have an engineering mind-set. You will therefore see lots of programmes geared around culture change or employee engagement that attempt to influence people in an overly ordered manner. Consultants will suggest and then implement "large group events", "focus groups" and "cascades". These happen to be very lucrative for the consultancies, but we will come back to that in Chapter 9. The real issue is that they tend to be planned with a specific end in mind, and so are still locked in cause and effect. To summarise a typical programme – "Our customers are unhappy, we need a more customer-focussed culture, let's take everyone through a customer focussed series of events." Whereas a less engineering ideology might say, "Our customers are unhappy, let's bring people together to try and solve it somehow or other."

Both of these approaches may look very similar; for example, they might both include large groups of people coming together for a period of time, but the ideology behind the second one is very hard to stomach. It relies on leaders trusting that the garden will grow but not knowing how. I personally had direct experience of this conflict when working with the large, blame-filled organisation that I mentioned earlier. The HR director was asking for my advice about how to address the toxicity of the culture. I suggested to her that we might want to bring together a large group of senior leaders to work on how they are leading the firm and the impact that method was having. My client was somewhat concerned. "What will the outputs be?" she asked. I told her that we might begin to get some shared views about their role in the culture. "No," she said. "What conclusions will they come to? We need to agree upfront which solutions we will lead them to, as we don't want them coming to conclusions that the top team disagrees with." We didn't end up working together on the project! She wanted a clear input and a clear output – cause and effect. As long as leaders ask for these things, they will find consultants who will provide them, even if they miss the point of how complex systems really work.

Most leadership books and consultants tell us to "Do this and you will succeed; if you don't believe me, look at Fred, he did it and he succeeded." Throughout this book, I have shown you many reasons why that thinking is flawed. At the heart of it is a belief that actions have impacts in a highly predictable way. Instead, we must accept that we are in organisations that are full of chaos, complexity, luck and randomness. If we accept this, we can still never guarantee success but we can at least increase its likelihood. Which neatly brings us to the next issue, that of success.

The Traditional View Of Business Success

Over the past few months, I have discussed this book with a range of colleagues and shown early chapters to a few. As I have pointed out some of the flaws in conventional thinking, they normally come back to me with the same question: "What does work then?" This has caused me to think deeply about what their question actually means. It has also highlighted to me what an important question it is to so many people: What worked? How you succeed is the killer question to the degree that we don't even realise that we are bound by it. Success – a solution "working" – seems to be the ultimate measure. "Does it work?" seems to trump every other question. People treat it as the ultimate test of worth. "Yes, yes," they say, "that all sounds very good in theory, but does it work?" If you wish to be grounded and in control, this really does seem to be the question to ask. However, like a 2D character seeing the inside of a sphere, I want to share with you an alternative way of seeing the world – a world where "Does it work?" may not be the most important question. Let's start at the beginning, however, with the conventional view of business success.

In many ways, business success is very straightforward. If business is about shareholder value then we can demonstrate success with a range of business metrics. The starting point for most people when they want to identify a successful business is likely to be one of the following:

- Revenue
- Revenue Growth
- Return on Investment
- Profitability
- Profit Growth
- Market Share

- Market Capitalisation
- Share Price
- Dividend Growth

Some of these can trade off against others, but if a business is balancing them well, or at least in the intended way, we would consider it successful and so look at what the leaders are doing to create this success. This in turn may lead us to a whole set of other measures that impact the financial ones, such as customer satisfaction and employee engagement. Very simple and easy to understand, but also very prone to the problems that I have identified earlier in this book.

In this world, our mission is to create sustainable business success. As leaders, we know that actions that lead to this success are good and actions that put it at risk are bad. So far, so simple.

The Ultimate Justification

Given the importance of these financial metrics, we increasingly see them being used to legitimise actions or activities that have a higher purpose. Take, for example, the issue of diversity in the workplace and, in particular, the role of women leaders. A typical study by Nancy M. Carter and Harvey M. Wagner (2011) makes the case very clearly. They found that Fortune 500 companies with three or more women in board positions created a competitive advantage over companies with no women on their boards. In particular, in the following three areas:

- Return on Sales: 84% advantage
- Return on Invested Capital: 60% advantage
- Return on Equity: 46% advantage

Rather uncharacteristically, I will turn off my normal cynicism about statistics and take these findings on face value. It certainly does seem to make a good case for diversity. Similar arguments are made for other noble causes. *Ethisphere* tells us that the world's most ethical companies' stocks have grown at twice the rate of the S&P 500. We hear how authentic leaders bring about great business results. For example, *HBR* cites the authenticity of Anne Mulcahy as being responsible for the trebling of the stock price of Xerox.

As I read back on the words I have written, I feel a curious mixture of delight and dismay. I am delighted that we can embrace diversity, act ethically and be authentic, and still achieve great business success. It makes me happy to live in a world where this is the case. However, the dismay I feel is that financial success has somehow become the measure of such things. Someone has felt the need to demonstrate these facts in order to give the behaviours legitimacy. If we are saying, "Look! Having women leaders on the board is good for business", aren't we in danger of becoming slaves to that rationale. If a study next week showed that a white male-dominated business had started to perform better, would that cause us to reject diversity? If unethical leaders improved share price, would that make it OK? If faking it rather than being authentic boosted sales, is that what we should advocate? Surely, we should embrace all of these things, regardless of whether they lead to "success", as measured by a narrow range of financial metrics.

Cracking the Code

As an interesting aside, my former employer, YSC, produced a research report on women in leadership called *Cracking the Code*. It was part of a project to increase the representation of women on the boards of UK companies. Among other things, the research discovered that financial business cases weren't very effective at persuading senior men to embrace diversity. They had all read the numbers above but hadn't been spurred to action. It turned out that the single biggest contributor to men embracing gender diversity was having a daughter. "Does it work?" was a less important question than "Is this the world I want my daughter to grow up in?"

The Third Metric

There has been another trend in recent years that has gone some way towards broadening our view of success. In *Thrive: The Third Metric to Redefining Success and Creating a Life of Well-Being, Wisdom, and Wonder*, Arianna Huffington argues that we need to go beyond the currently dominant measure of success, which she see as being money and power, and instead, focus on a third metric. Cynics will argue that it is easy for someone with lots of money and power to wax lyrical about a third metric, but at least she is saying it, and that can only be good. Huffington's third metric has four pillars: well-being, wisdom, wonder and giving. She rightly argues for a life with more balance and humanity, and urges us to have a different definition of success. While I applaud such attempts to broaden the definition of success, in some ways, I don't think that it goes far enough. We are still focussed on behaving some way as a means to an end. It may be happiness rather than money, but it still has the same dynamic.

As an alternative approach, I am tempted to focus on being the leader I want to be for its own sake, not because it gets me something in particular as a result. As a deep introvert and father of another, I was recently given Susan Cain's excellent *Quiet* by my long-suffering wife. As she discusses the rise of extraversion as a desirable state, precipitated by the work of Dale Carnegie, she reflects on the evolution of self-help books through the ages.

"Many of the earliest conduct guides were religious parables, like *The Pilgrim's Progress*, published in 1678, which warned readers to behave with restraint if they wanted to make it to heaven. The advice manuals of the nineteenth century were less religious but still preached the value of noble character. They featured case studies of historical heroes like Abraham Lincoln, revered not only as a gifted communicator but also as a modest man who did not, as Ralph Waldo Emerson put it, 'offend by superiority'. They also celebrated regular people who lived highly moral lives. A popular 1899 manual called *Character: The Grandest Thing in the World* featured a timid shop girl who gave away her meagre earnings to a freezing beggar, then rushed off before anyone could see what she'd done. Her virtue, the reader understood, derived not only from her generosity but also from her wish to remain anonymous.

"But by 1920, popular self-help guides had changed their focus from inner virtue to outer charm – 'to know *what* to say and *how* to say it,' as one manual put it. 'To create personality is power,' advised another. 'Try in every way to have command of the manners which make people think "he's a mighty likeable fellow,"' said a third. *Success* magazine and *The Saturday Evening Post* introduced departments instructing readers on the art of conversation. The same author, Orison Swett Marden, who wrote *Character: The Grandest Thing in the World* in 1899, produced another popular title in 1921. It was called *Masterful Personality*."

Later, she reports that the earlier guides used words like:

- Citizenship
- Duty
- Work
- Golden deeds
- Honour
- Reputation
- Morals
- Manners
- Integrity

While the later guides describe characteristics like:

- Magnetic
- Fascinating
- Stunning
- Attractive
- Glowing
- Dominant
- Forceful
- Energetic

While Cain makes a point about introversion and extraversion, I think that she also highlights a trend from being of good character as an end in its own right to simply behaving in a way that is going to maximise your likelihood of success. In *Return on Character: The Real Reason Leaders and Their Companies Win*, Fred Kiel claims that people with his definition of character achieve five times the return on assets than those without. Even if his research was not prone to the many issues laid out in this book (which I doubt) then character is still just being packaged as a technique for being successful, and so by my definition, this is not character at all. True character persists regardless of failure, not simply to earn success.

When I talk to people outside of the work context, I think that people do still value character in its own right. I would love to be seen as a good man, as a man of integrity, and I am sure I am not alone in this desire. I am also not alone in failing at times to meet that aspiration. But somehow, in the world of business, the dialogue so easily turns to success as the ultimate measure. We can recognise leaders who succeed and happen to be good, but we are equally in awe of those who just succeed. There is precious little narrative of those who are good, even though circumstances led to failure. The interesting thing for me is that, by doing all the right things, I can influence, but not control, my success. On the other hand, I can entirely control whether or not I act with integrity. I will try my best to succeed, but if I fail, I at least want the consolation that I didn't lose my principles along the way.

Conclusion

Throughout this book, we have seen how those who offer us recipes for success are often doomed to failure. The complexity of the world shows many ways to both succeed and fail. I am encouraged than many noble behaviours can lead to success, but we must acknowledge that they can also fail. Likewise, some morally questionable activities might get you the results you want. This chapter has shown that cause and effect is questionable at least and certainly unpredictable. It really is hard to tell a leader what they can do in order to achieve success. I now ask you to go one step further and ask yourself what kind of leader you want to be, *independently* of whether it leads to success. If we could learn to value character as much as we do success, might that not be a better way to live. We should not be afraid to put morality above success and act accordingly. Ed Catmull puts it well:

> "I know one gaming company in Los Angeles that had a stated goal of turning over 15 per

cent of its workforce every year. The reasoning behind such a policy was that production shoots up when you hire smart, hungry kids straight out of school and work them to death. Attrition was inevitable under such conditions, but that was okay, because the company's needs outweighed those of the worker. Did it work? Sure, maybe. To a point. But if you ask me, that kind of thing is not just misguided, it is immoral."

To close, let me reassure you that I am not in any way against success. I like it very much. However, I know that it is a hard thing to guarantee, and anyone who tells you they have the answer is mistaken. I also know that it is not the most important thing in the world. Being able to live with myself and the way I have behaved is. Throughout the rest of this book, I will explore how to be the best version of yourself, the person you want to be, while at the same time, leading your business in a way that increases its chances of success (however defined) without necessarily being able to guarantee it.

References

Adams, S. (2013) *How to Fail at Almost Everything and Still Win Big*

Cain, S. (2012) *Quiet: The Power Of Introverts In A World That Can't Stop Talking*

Carter, N. M. and Wagner, H. M. (2011) *The Bottom Line: Corporate Performance and Women's Representation on Boards, 2004-2008*

RED PILL: THE TRUTH ABOUT LEADERSHIP

Catmull, E. (2014) *Creativity, Inc. Overcoming the Unseen Forces that Stand in the Way of True Innovation*

George, B., Sims, P., McLean, A. and Mayer, N. (2007*) Discovering Your Authentic Leadership, Harvard Business Review, February 2007*

Huffington, A. (2014) *Thrive: The Third Metric to Redefining Success and Creating a Happier Life*

Kiel, F. (2015) *Return on Character: The Real Reason Leaders and Their Companies Win*

Skinner, B. F. (1948) The Superstition of the Pigeon *Journal of Experimental Psychology*, April 1948

Pascale, R. T., Middleman, M. and Gioja, L. (2000) *Surfing The Edge Of Chaos: The Laws Of Nature And The New Laws Of Business*

Chapter 7
Too Much Of A Good Thing:
How All Strengths Can Be Overdone

*"There comes a time when you look into the mirror and you
realize that what you see is all that you will ever be.
And then you accept it. Or you kill yourself.
Or you stop looking in mirrors."*
Tennessee Williams

The RBS Story

The Royal Bank of Scotland was founded in 1727 and
was far from aggressive in expanding itself. It took more
than a century to open an office in London, and another
100 years before it really started to grow south of the
border. All that changed in 2000, when Fred Goodwin
took over as CEO. Within a year, he had pulled off one
of the most amazing deals the banking world had seen.
He managed to buy UK giant, NatWest – which was
three times its size – for £21 billion. Fred Goodwin was
named Businessman of the Year by *Forbes* magazine
for what it described as a "brilliantly strategized hostile
takeover" of NatWest.

However, this coup was just the beginning. Acquisitions of Royal Insurance, Churchill Insurance and Char-

ter One were among the major deals that followed. In one year alone (2003), there were seven more deals that steadily pushed RBS up the league table of Big Banks. Under Goodwin's leadership, RBS opened offices in Asia, across Europe, the Irish Republic, and the US. It even bought a 5% stake in the Bank of China. Goodwin and RBS seemed to be the masters of acquisition and growth. They had a strength and knew how to use it.

Things began to unravel in 2007 when RBS learned that arch-rival Barclays were negotiating to buy ABN Amro. Despite signs that the global money markets were stretched, RBS went head-to-head with Barclays to deny them their prize. Then came the banking crisis, triggered by the fall of Lehman Brothers in the US. Confidence in British banks slumped because of their exposure to the US subprime mortgage crisis, and share prices collapsed as it became clear that many of the assets against which RBS and others had borrowed money were now worth only a fraction of their previous value. The bank was only saved from total collapse by a bailout from the British Government.

Everything in Moderation

The supreme strength of RBS – its ability to acquire other banks – was its ultimate undoing. This should have come as no surprise. Goodwin himself once said, "The key to good deal-making is knowing when to walk away", but seemed to ignore his own advice. There are many lessons to learn from the story of RBS, but in this chapter, we will focus on just one: the strengths of an organisation, or individual, can always be overdone to the point that they cause harm. We see this easily in every story of failure, but it is much less likely to be mentioned in the realm of success stories. Typically, our management books tell us stories of success that often focus on an underlying strength of the leader or organisation in question. We may hear about the buying power of Walmart, the emotional connectivity of Apple or Amazon's business model. Perhaps, if we could copy some of these strengths, we could be successful too. Perhaps we could.

The problem is that we are hearing about organisational strengths at a point when they appear to be working, and it is tempting to think that, with any strength, more will always be better. Surely, some might think, you can't have too much buying power or too much emotional connection with your customers. However, I would contend that maybe you can. Maybe it is possible to overuse all strengths. Might it be possible to have so much buying power that you inadvertently destroy suppliers who then rebel? Of course it is. Might it be possible to have such emotional connection with customers that you begin to rely on that affection, so neglect other things? I think so. If, no matter how great the strength, it is possible to overuse it, then any simple formula that encourages you to copy a good thing as much as you can, for as long as you can, might be propelling you towards disaster.

For the sake of simplicity, most textbooks tell us the things that we should be doing with clear stories and lessons. The things that are being advocated are almost universally good things. They are undoubtedly strengths, but often, too little time is given to considering how much is just right. Indeed, it often doesn't seem to occur to the writer to raise the subject. Take two of the most obvious strengths that organisations must develop; customer focus and employee engagement. The case for both of these attributes is overwhelming. In addition, many businesses need to increase them – a lot. No surprise then that few people feel it necessary to take the time to warn against too much customer focus or too much employee engagement. However, in the real world, the best managers and leaders that I work with completely understand that these strengths must be kept in balance with other factors, not least cost management.

A few years ago, I was invited to an award ceremony that was recognising businesses with great employee engagement. Employers tried to outgun each other with a range of free massages, beanbag-filled brainstorming rooms and regular sabbaticals for grateful employees. The business that I had been consulting for was not the winner, but the event was worth attending just to hear the winner's speech. The emotional recipient took the stage and, after thanking judges, noted the poignancy of the timing. "It is fantastic to receive this prize in my last week in the company, as unfortunately, we have had to wind the business up."

Business life is a difficult and complex balancing act, but too much business advice is framed in simple and easy terms. Perhaps we need to spend more time helping leaders deal with the complex, subtle and changing balancing act that is business and less time shouting simplistic mantras. I sometimes see leaders as brave souls in the circus, walking the perilous high wire. Down below, there are armies of consultants. Some are shouting, "Lean right else you will fall left", while others squeal, "No, read my new book – *The power of left-leaning*." None of these things provides what the tightrope walker really needs – balance and belief.

Leadership Development – Quiz Time

Here is a quick quiz for you. Which of the following four options most closely reflect your own personal philosophy of development?

1. You should play to your strengths. Figure out where you are better than others, then become truly exceptional at these things. Find roles that play to your strengths.
2. You should eliminate weaknesses. Find out where you are not as good as other leaders and then practice until you are.
3. You should reframe your weaknesses. If you are bad at something, with the best will in the world, you will never be a star at it, so find a way of making it an asset. If the world gives you lemons, make lemonade
4. Beware of overplaying your strengths. All strengths can become a weakness. Learn to manage the volume control of your strength so that you don't overdo it.

If you are anything like me, you will be torn, as you see some merit in more than one of these options. Maybe you will endorse all of them. However, the business world is largely composed of advocates of one approach over another. Over the coming pages,

I will attempt to make the best case possible for each of these four philosophies – forgive me if I contradict myself, I am genuinely trying to advocate on behalf of each approach. Please don't take these arguments as my own views (although some of them are).

Philosophy 1: Playing To Strengths

In the 90s, a typical leadership training course might have involved a participant finding out how they compared to good leaders, identifying where they fell short, then working to bridge those gaps. But in 2001, Marcus Buckingham and Donald Clifton wrote the bestseller, *Now, Discover Your Strengths*, that put forward a strength-based approach that has since been enthusiastically taken up by leadership developers around the world. The Gallup organisation have taken things further in producing tests that help leaders identify which of 34 "talent themes" you might have as your greatest strength. By identifying your strengths in this way, you are then in a position to make the most of them. Why struggle to excel in an area where you lack gifts, when instead, you can celebrate what comes naturally and find a role that really plays on it. By recognising that people have different gifts, we can avoid turning people into leadership clones and instead, enjoy a rich diversity of talents. Rather than trying to be good at everything, I simply need to work with colleagues whose strengths are complementary to my own. Not only is it more efficient, but also, each individual feels the glow of being able to bring unique value. It is simple as putting the round pegs in round holes.

Leaders often ask me about how to boost their chances of promotion, given the strengths that they have. I will then get them to reflect on how a promotion decision might get made by a CEO. I think it is unlikely that he or she will say, "You know what, Bill there has no obvious weaknesses, let's put him on the executive team," however, I have often heard a CEO say, "We really need Jill around the top table, nobody has the same customer insight as her and we are really feeling the lack of it." The blunt truth may be that "spikey" people, people with pronounced strengths, are more likely to progress, because their unique skill will stand out and they will instantly make a difference to any team they join. Sure, those strengths may come with a downside, but maybe that is a price worth paying. How can the perfectly-rounded leader ever hope to make the same kind of difference?

Playing to strengths isn't just about trading on what you have, however; it is also about taking them further. There are a number of ways in which you can do this:

1. If you are good at something, try to be great.
2. If you are great within your function, take that greatness to the rest of the business.
3. Teach your skill to others.
4. Create a whole organisational culture that reflects your strengths.

It is not just in the realm of leadership that this thinking can apply. I know full well that I will never make it as an elite sprinter; no matter how much I had trained as a child, I never would. I just don't have the body for it. With training, I could be less hopeless; alternatively, I could dedicate myself to a walk of life where I stand a fighting chance of success. Getting hung up on what we can't do is futile – much better to focus on what we can.

Philosophy 2: Eliminating Weaknesses

Leading a business is not a single skill; it involves a wide range of capabilities, from influencing people, through commercial understanding, to organisational and project skills. This list could go on and on. We know that not everyone will excel at everything, but most organisations will identify a dozen or so competencies that are critical to success in that particular business. Like a carpenter who needs to use a hammer as skilfully as a lathe, there are a range of skills that need to be built before you can move from apprentice to master. If a carpenter cannot drill wood effectively, then he needs to learn; he cannot simply play to his hammer-wielding strengths. Likewise, leaders who cannot motivate people need to address this weakness and not just celebrate their exceptional project management skills. A chain is only as strong as its weakest link; likewise, lacking a vital leadership skill can undermine greatness elsewhere.

Those that are critical of this philosophy will make the point that people may have a natural talent in one area or another, and it is therefore futile to try to build a skill where you lack one. "I am never going to be a sprinter," they say, "I'm just not built that way so why try to be something I am not." However, recent research suggests that this thinking is limiting. With enough practice, it is possible to develop a whole range of skills. In *Bounce*, Matthew Syed tells us the story of László Polgár, the educational psychologist who, despite not being a player himself, turned all his daughters into chess champions as a way of proving this point. Of course, this took many years of hard work, and that may be why this philosophy proves unpopular. Isn't it more cosy and reassuring to be told, "Don't worry about that weakness, just do what you do well," instead of the harsher truth of, "Like it or not, being good at this is part of the job, so start practising."

It is not necessary to be a champion at everything, but you do need to be good enough at the things that are essential. It is therefore vital to identify where you have a weakness – where you operate at a level that is below the expectations of the role. We don't tolerate carpenters who can't drill, gardeners who can't dig, or pilots who can't land. Why then should it be acceptable to have a leader who can't inspire? Critics may argue that competence-based approaches lead to clones that lack character, but this doesn't need to be the case. Learning the basic skills of your job does not remove your personality. The important thing to remember is that you can have all the skills in the world, but if you bring your greatest weakness into the room too, you can be sure that this will be the thing that people remember about you.

When I was eight years old, my school took my class for a music test to decide who should be taught an instrument. I was duly played a series of notes and was asked to identify which was a semitone higher than which. Perhaps because I didn't even know what "a semitone higher" meant, perhaps because instruments were not played in my house, perhaps because my ability to discern tones was not developed, I bombed the test and never learned to play an instrument or even read music. I am musically illiterate. In the same school, I was also told in a public way that I absolutely cannot sing. That set the course for my life. The teachers proved themselves right – I still cannot sing or read music. My own son is now eight, and when he plays the piano, it brings tears to my eyes. I sit next to him as he plays every evening. I cannot guide him in any way, as his capabilities far exceed my own – but I sit there anyway. Did we test to see if he had a "gift" before starting the lessons? Of course not. We knew that he, like every other child around, could learn if given the opportunity. Weaknesses can be overcome – perhaps it is finally time for me to learn to play the piano too.

Philosophy 3: Reframe Weaknesses

Bold risk-takers will look at rigorous analysers and accuse them of analysis paralysis. Critical evaluators might view the highly empathic as weak and subjective. Creatives may see empiricists as lacking imagination. It is not just beauty that is in the eye of the beholder – so too is weakness. We like to label those who are different to us in derogatory terms, perhaps to make ourselves feel better, probably because we genuinely find it hard to see the value of that different approach. Take the left-handed among us. Right-handers might frame left-handedness as a weakness that creates disadvantages when it comes to corkscrews and the like, but fortunately, we have long ago abandoned trying to beat right-handedness into our children. We now accept and value the difference. Why then do we try to create an army of leaders who are all the same and reject those that do not fit the mould?

Weakness is just another way of saying "different to the way I want you to be". Instead of just accepting such judgment, wouldn't it be better to identify what is of value in that supposed weakness and then make the most of the difference that you possess? David Rendall makes the case in what he calls *The Freak Factor: Discovering Uniqueness by Flaunting Weakness*. He believes that, like Rudolph the Red Nosed Reindeer, while the other reindeer might laugh and call you names, a wise Santa lets you use it to guide his sleigh at night. Any of the weaknesses on the left of the table should not be eliminated; rather they should be celebrated and nurtured for the strength on the right that they bring.

We have limited time and energy for self-development; we should therefore not waste it by going against our true nature. Rather we would work out how to get the best out of what is different and distinctive about us.

APPARENT WEAKNESS	CORRESPONDING STRENGTH
Unorganised	Creative
Inflexible	Organised

Stubborn	Dedicated
Inconsistent	Flexible
Emotionless	Calm
Negative	Realistic
Weak	Humble

Philosophy 4: Avoid Overplaying Strengths

In most organisations, managers face the annual performance appraisal ritual and, across a range of measures, they will be asked if a direct report is "not meeting expectations", "meeting expectations", or "exceeding expectations". Similarly, employees of all types frequently complete 360-degree feedback evaluations on their colleagues, in which they are asked to judge behaviours on a negative to positive scale. The scale may go from "a significant weakness" through to "a significant strength", or it may take the form of a frequency judgment from "never" to "always". What is lacking in all of these evaluations is the concept of "too much". The scales implicitly suggest that more is always better, but is that really true? What would happen if you gave the option of rating someone as overdoing a strength? Well that is exactly what Kaplan and Kaiser have done with their *Leadership Versatility Index*. Unsurprisingly, when this option is made available, leaders are frequently rated as overdoing a strength.

In some ways, it is surprising that it has taken so long for this realisation to gain traction, as the concept of overdone strengths is deeply embedded in our culture. The image of the muscle-bound giant inadvertently breaking a chair or a cup appears in many books, plays and films. The stock phrase in response to such an accident is always the same: "Sorry, he doesn't know his own strength." Let's just dwell on that for a moment. How many times at work might we see a leader and be able to say, "He doesn't know his own strength." If you think about it, it is much more often they may initially be apparent. The leader who uses her great intellect to destroy the arguments of all-comers. The boss whose precision and detail orientation allows them to analyse everything to the nth degree. The CEO whose charisma makes even the most hare-brained plans sound compelling. Forget weaknesses, what you really need to worry about is your strengths.

In the same way that Philosophy 3 can rebrand all weaknesses as strengths, it is possible to overuse all strength to the point of weakness. If you are too flexible, you become inconsistent. If you are too decisive, you may be stubborn. At some point or another, with virtually every leader I have coached, I have had reason to say, "Your charisma/intellect/rigour/creativity (delete as applicable) is like a hugely powerful engine – you don't need to drive it at full throttle all the time." Strengths are to be valued, but unless they are driven with finesse, they become like out of control vehicles.

Which Philosophy?

So, I have done my best to make the case for each of these philosophies. Apologies if you are a devotee of one of them and feel I have misrepresented your view. So the obvious question is which one is right? In preparation for this chapter, I have asked a number of people for their views on which philosophy is best and have had three types of response. The first is a kneejerk "all of the above" answer, as that always sounds like a good bet. The second answer comes from people who spot the inconsistency of some of the philosophies. Philosophies 1 and 3 can sit quite nicely together, as if you pursue them, you end up with more "spikey" characters, whereas Philosophies 2 and 4 combine to help build leaders who are more "rounded". It seems hard to simultaneously believe that leaders should be spikey and rounded at the same time, so people plump for one or the other. The third type of answer is that only one Philosophy is right and it just happens to be the Philosophy behind my own company's latest product. We will cover more on this particular problem in Chapter 9.

Which type of respondent am I? Well, despite having dismissed their views as easy and kneejerk, I think that I am in the first camp. There really is some merit in each of the four approaches, and I have made use of each at some point or another. I have encouraged some people to play to their strengths and warned others to tone them down. I have advised some leaders to overcome a weakness while encouraging others to accept their limitations. Does that make my philosophy inconsistent? Maybe, but if there is anything that I have learned, it is that any fixed philosophy of leadership, any model that claims to be the truth, will always fail in some context or other. It is therefore context that should determine which approach needs to be taken. By advocating one or two approaches, you will be exposed when the other way of thinking is what is required. If there is merit in all approaches, the big problem becomes knowing which approach to take at any one point in time.

Know Thyself

Of all the attributes that seem vital to success in life and leadership, self-insight has to be up there among the most important. If we are really aware of our own strengths and weaknesses and, crucially, the impact that they are having, then we are able to adjust our behaviour accordingly. What strengths do I have? When should I prize them and when should I fear them? Where are my weaknesses? Must I commit to improve them or recognise that they are part of my distinctiveness as a human being? These are such important questions to answer that we rarely manage to do so alone. Accordingly, the business of leadership feedback is booming. For modern leaders, the feedback is coming thick and fast. They have their performance appraised by bosses. Psychometric assessments seem to be everywhere. They have 360-degree feedback forms completed by peers, direct reports, customers, and even family and friends. Once a year, a pile of employee engagement data will hit the desk, and, if they are very unlucky, they will pay a visit to someone like me for a formal leadership appraisal. One would think that with all this feedback flying around, we would have already built a generation of super-leaders.

Don't get me wrong. I am a big fan of feedback mechanisms, but like everything, they can be both overdone and, at the same time, insufficient. The typical leader I see today is noticeably more sophisticated than those I first encountered in the early 90s. Expectations of managers as motivators of others has increased, and those in such roles have risen to the challenge, yet recent years have also seen some of the worst stories of leadership failure imaginable. An environment rich in feedback has problems as well as advantages, as we will see in the next chapter. In the meantime, let me make a few points about getting the best of feedback.

1. It is not enough to know how you are perceived – you must also care.
2. It is not enough to care about how you are perceived – you must be ready and able to change.
3. How you are perceived is only part of the story. I can be seen as a caring boss while, at the same time, my employees are suffering from more and more stress.

This last point is especially interesting to me. What is more important – being a commercially astute leader or making a profit? Is it better to be loved by customers or have them continue to buy your products? Clearly, we always say both, and that they are connected, but it is easy for a leader to end up focussing so much on themselves and how they are seen that they lose sight of why they need to be seen that way in the first place. A feedback mechanism is vital when it comes to steering anything that is on the move. Given the nature of complexity and chaos, you cannot simply pre-programme a course of action and expect it to work. You need a feedback mechanism to tell the drone that it is flying too high or too low, too far to port or too far to starboard. Similarly, we cannot say that this or that is the perfect way to run a business and then just execute it. We therefore need feedback mechanisms to tell us whether we are on track and whether we need to adjust. The challenge is to know which feedback to use. What measures matter and what source is reliable?

Conclusion

While we started with the story of RBS, most of this chapter has been about individual leadership. However, I think that all the points that have been made can apply at the organisational level too. Depending on the context, an organisation can overdo a strength or not play to it enough. At times, it needs to change its competences; at other times, it needs to accept its limitations? Pursuing just one philosophy is unlikely to be a sensible thing to do. As always, the problem is knowing which one to use when. Like individual leaders, organisations benefit from rich feedback mechanisms, but there is a risk associated with attending to the wrong sort of feedback.

In the next chapter, we will explore feedback in all its forms – for individual leaders and for whole organisations. We will see both the benefits and the pitfalls of being observed.

References

Buckingham, M. and Clifton, D. (2001) *Now, Discover Your Strengths*

Kaplan, R. E. and Kaiser, R. B. (2013) *Fear Your Strengths: What You Are Best At Could Be Your Biggest Problem*

Chapter 8
Hall Of Mirrors:
The Impact Of Observation On
The Observed

*"Woe to you, when all people speak well of you,
for so their fathers did to the false prophets."*
Luke 6:2

Yahoo!

Jerry Yang is the co-founder of Yahoo! (at one time the most popular search engine in the world). When Microsoft made a bid to buy them in 2008, they offered a whopping $44.6 billion. This was around 62% more than their market valuation. For most shareholders, it seemed like a no-brainer, but to Jerry Yang, it wasn't enough. For whatever reason – false belief in the future, pride or arrogance – he kept saying "no". Not only did the share price take a massive hit following this decision, but so too did sales and, in short order, the company was worth a fraction of what Microsoft had offered. It didn't take long for Jerry to be shown the door by his board of directors.

This chapter will explore this tendency for successful people to detach themselves from reality. To the rest of the world, Jerry had been made a great offer, but his belief in the brilliance and future of Yahoo! far exceeded the available data. We will explore the pride and hubris that drives management decisions like this, then move on to the standard "cure" for this condition – the provision of feedback.

Hubris

The corporate illness of our time has been dubbed "New Head Office Syndrome". It describes how vibrant IT start-ups suddenly seem to lose their lustre when they become successful enough to build a shiny, new head office. Others suggest that the best way to bring on disaster is to win an award or be listed as a role model organisation. Suddenly, you are spending your time showing visitors around and explaining, with great pride, how you have figured out the secret of success. If everyone is telling you how great you are, it is a very easy message to believe, but potentially a dangerous one too, as you may begin to forget what really matters in your organisation and what has brought you success in the first place.

If this tendency can afflict a whole organisation, it is possible for it to become especially acute among the most senior managers. In addition to the external adulation, they will also have the reverence and praise of their people to deal with. The role also comes with high levels of power over other people – a notoriously difficult gift to contend with. Whether it be Pittacus – "Office shows the man" – or Lord Acton – "Power tends to corrupt and absolute power corrupts absolutely"

– we have always been made aware of the damaging effects of having power over people.

Even if they do not go to the extreme of outright megalomania, any person in power – who is achieving success – will begin to feel the effects of the power that they have. I was recently talking to a newly-appointed managing director of a successful company who came to me with some distress, as she was already beginning to feel herself losing empathy for the people she led. The intensity of the job, the pressure to meet numerical targets, and the challenge of winning people over were all beginning to erode her sympathy for the plight of the people she led. They soon became one her challenges, rather than people who could help. At the same time, she was beginning to need to rely on policies, procedures and statistics to manage people, as she now had too many people to consult personally. As this happens, it becomes harder and harder to retain empathy with people. It is easy to set a policy on the limits of sick leave, but harder to face a colleague who has been diagnosed with a chronic disease and worries about their family finances. Slowly but surely, a leader can begin to see people as numbers rather than individuals.

At the same time that her connection to people as individuals was starting to erode, whenever her staff engaged with her, they seemed to have a problem or a complaint. Issue after issue was being delegated up to her desk. No wonder leaders so quickly start to say, "Don't bring me problems, bring me solutions." The sheer emotional pressure of so many problems being brought to your door is a huge strain, but as we saw in Chapter 2, sometimes the people bringing these problems are actually trying to warn us about a cliff that lies ahead. For lots of very understandable reasons, the first victim of increased power appears to be the reduction in listening.

A Failure To Listen

Founded in 1962 by Sam Walton, Walmart is one of the most successful companies in the world. Their retail expertise has enabled them to open 11,000 stores in 28 countries. One would assume that what they don't know about retail isn't worth knowing. Back in 1997, they took this expertise into Germany, following the acquisition of Wertkauf and Interspar. However, on this occasion, things did not go according to plan. In 2006, they were forced to quit and pull out, and we may never know the cost of this failed endeavour.

In the intervening years, analysts have pored over the reason why their success formula failed to work. Their approach clearly worked outside the US, as had been shown in a range of other overseas ventures. What was the issue with Germany? A range of possibilities have been suggested. Employees being expected to chant WALMART in the morning didn't go down well, and customers rebelled against how discounts and pricing was arranged and the time it took to shop in store. There may even have been a mismatch between German expectations of ecological protection and the Walmart approach. However, these are not just opinions that have been formed with the benefit of hindsight. Criticisms like this were levelled at the time by the company's own employees.

Local management and front-line workers understood the German consumer much better that their US bosses, but one can only assume that the certainty that senior executives had in the Walmart success formula meant that they closed their ears to these objections and pressed ahead with the Walmart way. If only the top management of Walmart could have had the same insight as their German staff, who knows how the story could have ended.

Feedback To The Rescue

If ever there was a panacea that was touted around the business world as the cure for all ills, it must be feedback. Feedback can keep us honest, it tells us how we are really perceived, it tells us what is working and what isn't. It is the essential tool in the kitbag of every leader. The theory goes that if only someone were able to provide us with an honest mirror, we would be able to see where we were going wrong and put it right. It doesn't just need to be feedback on how we are listening; every aspect of business and leadership can be improved by gaining a better understanding of how others see us. Whether we are seeking it from our clients or our staff, we have increasingly sophisticated tools for helping us learn what people think of us. Focusing in on employees, two of the most popular feedback techniques are employee engagement surveys and 360-degree feedback surveys.

Most large organisations that I know embark on an annual employee engagement survey. The whole company is polled for their opinions on a wide range of subjects related to their experience as an employee. The questions are often standard ones that allow the organisation to compare its level of employee engagement with that of other businesses. If 50% of people say that they are dissatisfied with pay, we can quickly see if that is more or less than usual in other businesses, and so we will know how to act accordingly. Normally, the results can be broken down by country or department, so that individual leaders can see how well they are engaging their people and how their scores have changed over time.

360-degree feedback gives an even more personal-ised sense of how you are doing. This method involves you nominating a small number of people who know you well. These people are asked all about your per-sonal style of leadership, what works well and what doesn't. It is a pretty scary process to be evaluated in such a focussed way, but it is hard to find a modern leader who has not gone through the ordeal. It seems we live in a blessed time where we are all feedback-rich. Why then do we seem to be making the same, or even bigger, mistakes than the past? Feedback makes complete logical sense – it should be the answer, and it must be the answer – so why isn't it working?

Feedback Gone Wrong

My very first experience of the feedback process going wrong happened at the end of my time with the now-departed Nortel. Post-merger restructuring had led to the closure of my department and I was being laid off, but rather than simply leave the business, a senior manager suggested an alternative. "We just received a whole pile of customer feedback," he said. "Why don't you stay on for another three months and analyse it for us?" Well this sounded pretty good to me while I job-hunted, so I agreed and set about the task. The feedback turned out to be exceptionally damning and criticised just about every part of our business, but I faithfully analysed and organised it all into a simple, punchy presentation.

When my work was done, three months later, I was asked to present via video-conference (a very new technology then) to the most senior stakeholder in Canada. Her face filled the screen in front of me as she patiently listened to my no-holds-barred critique. When I had finished, she said, "That's great, Paul, now I have a few people here who may have some questions." She then leaned forward to press a button. The camera zoomed out to reveal a whole boardroom full of people. Lined up on either side were the heads of each and every department that I had just trashed. I had never seen an angrier mob in my life. I suddenly realised why the guy who was leaving the company anyway had been given this particular project. Nobody who wanted any chance of promotion would make themselves so unpopular with the most senior and influential players in the business. Clearly, this leader had pulled a particularly mean and underhand trick, but at least it was one that got the truth out. Had I known that all those people were listening, I am sure that I would have been tempted to be more diplomatic and so risked losing the power of the feedback.

One of the problems with feedback is that it can sometimes be very hard to take. We all know this, so soften the blow when we can. The phrase "Don't shoot the messenger" comes from our absolute awareness of the risks of being honest. Whistle-blower laws are now put in place to encourage the reporting of truly unethical behaviour, but for regular feedback, it is easiest to pull punches and let people save face. It is a really difficult thing to do to give someone really honest feedback. If there is a chance that I will receive a negative response and if I don't care that much about the success or failure of the leader in question, will I really have the courage to be honest?

Later in my career, I noticed a similar effect when working with struggling senior executives. On one occasion, I was called in by a business that wanted me to work with a senior leader to help him understand the 360-degree feedback that he was about to receive as part of his annual review. His boss gave me a briefing in which he laid out, in no uncertain terms, the damage that this person was doing. By the sound of things, this person had upset all his colleagues and was close to being dismissed. He was in the last-chance saloon and they wanted me to help him process things. Two weeks later, the 360-degree feedback report was sent to me ahead of meeting the faltering executive in question. I read the report with a growing sense of disbelief. It was bland and neutral. Ratings were OK and none of the comments mentioned anything the manager had told me. In fact, the line manager's own comments (which were clearly marked) were as politely positive as the rest. Like a reluctant firing squad, it seems that everyone had hoped someone else was going to load the live round.

Other Feedback Issues

While the main issue with feedback systems is that people don't like either receiving or giving it (despite what they claim), there are a range of other problems that can be encountered. Many of these stem from our tendency to want to give a numerical measure to feedback rather than accept qualitative comments. I will often see 360-degree feedback with no words at all, only ratings of different behaviours; likewise, employee engagement surveys consist of endless charts of numbers and customer feedback is reduced to a single "Net Promoter Score" (NPS). The reason for doing this seems reasonable enough. By expressing feedback as a number, we are able to track progress over time and compare the feedback that we receive to that of competitors. In consequence, however, a number of feedback flaws emerge.

1. **Loss of information** – Inevitably, when a complex feeling is expressed as a number, some of that complexity is lost. If asked about someone influencing style, I might describe in words some of the contradictions in a person's character, but if I need to give it a 1 to 10 rating then such subtlety is lost. Further numeric manipulations may lose even more data. Take the previously-mentioned NPS. Customers will rate their likelihood to recommend your services to a friend on a 1 to 10 scale. A rating of 9 or 10 is considered Positive, 7 or 8 is Neutral, and 1-6 is Negative. You simply subtract the number of negative ratings from the positive ones to get your score. This neat, little metric – expressed

as a percentage – is the basis of huge numbers of bonus schemes and corporate objectives. While this approach brings many benefits, you can't get around the fact that someone scoring you a 1 is regarded the same as someone who scores you a 6. Important data has been lost.

2. **False maths** – Laid on top of this simplification issue is the fact that somewhat dubious mathematics is often applied to feedback scores. On a typical 360-degree feedback form, you may well be asked to rate someone on a scale where 1 = Never, 2 = Rarely, 3 = Sometimes, 4 = Often, and 5 = Always (or something similar). Once this is done, people then treat the numbers as numbers rather than replacements for words and then add, subtract or average them. So if you have one person say that you *Never* listen to them (1) while someone else tells you that you *Always* listen (5), you will get the same average score (3) as if two people had both said you *Sometimes* listen (3). But, to my mind, there is a big difference between sometimes listening to everyone versus selectively listening to some and ignoring others.

3. **Rating chasing** – Flawed as it may be, once feedback has been expressed as a numeric rating, the problems really start. The numbers are put into bonus schemes as a way of driving performance. Rather than being rewarded for improving customer service, business leaders will be incentivised to raise NPS. While these may sound like the same thing, they are actually quite different. If my objective is to

change a number, I will focus on changing a number, not necessarily on the intent behind that number. In the NPS case, I may give up on the "1" raters and instead focus on the neutral 8s and try to make them positive 9s. By doing this, I will more easily change the all-important NPS and I will also have improved the experience of some customers, but I will have missed the important concerns of other customers as they don't impact the metric so easily.

Ways of manipulating a metric without really changing what it is supposed to represent are manifold. For example, some of my early career was spent as a management trainer, and at the end of every session, we doled out the "happy sheets". These were surveys of satisfaction with the training that had to be completed by course attendees. Early on, I saw the most shameless and funny manipulation of this approach to receiving feedback. Imagine the scene – our courses were run in therapy style circles, no tables, just a ring of chairs. My co-tutor handed out the forms and then placed a small table in the middle of the room. "Please fill out the forms," he said, "then place them on the table in the middle." We waited patiently as people scribbled and eventually, the first person completed and placed her form on the table. To everyone's surprise, with a great flourish, my colleague picked up the piece of paper and began to read what everyone had assumed would be confidential feedback. He occasionally looked up and eyed the woman who had written it. The atmosphere in the room changed in an instant, as realisation dawned on the others. Ever so gently, you could just make out people erasing their previous entries and putting something more flattering instead. My colleague never heard the truth, but he sure did come top of the customer satisfaction league table.

4. **Tunnel vision** – Once the metric has been chosen, then it is very easy for it to become the only thing that people focus on. People will often say that, if you want to change something, you have to measure it. That is, unfortunately, all too true – the only things you end up changing are the things you are measuring – but great leadership is often defined by the things that you do beyond or between the behaviours that are formally measured.

Mirror, Mirror On The Wall

Earlier, we touched on the problem of giving senior people the honest truth. It should therefore not be surprising to find that senior people are often told what they want to hear, or at least to be kept away from negative messages. In truth, I don't think that I see much false praise of leaders; I don't really hear people lavishing an incompetent boss with praise. That particular style of ingratiating follower only seems to appear in the movies. What I do see, however, is a tendency to carefully manage and spin information that flows upwards. This is particularly true of leaders who pride themselves on being tough and demanding. I have come across several different businesses where people who are going to present to the top team can reasonably expect a mauling. In one business, visitors to the executive team were not even allowed to sit down. They would stand and present their business results, then the exceptionally intelligent CEO would find any flaw in what he saw and use it to destroy the speaker. Once word of this approach got out, you can imagine the impact that it had on later visitors. Whatever you do, they were told, don't give him any ammunition to attack you. The result was that he got to hear less and less bad news and more and more reports that the decisions he had made and projects he had initiated were going very well.

So what happens to someone who finds themselves being praised and reinforced at every turn? Might they begin to believe that they really are a great leader who has all the answers? You bet they do. Sometimes it seems that feedback, the cure to the problem of self-insight, actually makes the problem worse when the feedback being received is a distortion of the truth. We started this chapter by looking at the problems of leaders lacking self-insight and so becoming arrogant. The cure of feedback would be great if it worked, but all too often, the feedback that these people receive is so positive or confused that it leaves them with even less self-insight than they started with. If it was just the leader that was at risk, it would be bad enough, but sometimes, the whole moral framework of an organisation is put in peril.

Slippery Slopes

To give ourselves a reality check, we often bring in external agencies to tell us the "real" truth. If my own people might be shy or scared, let's hire a consultancy to tell us how it really is. We can then say, with pride, that our approach has been externally audited. Well, the Enron saga teaches us that even external agencies may be as inclined to tell us what we want to hear as our own, but sometimes the effect is less obviously criminal and is more subtle and slow to come about. Gino describes an interesting experiment that shows us how.

In this experiment, two roles were assigned – that of estimator and auditor. The estimator (who was in fact a secret experimenter) made a guess of how many pennies were in a jar. The auditor had to either approve that estimate or dispute it. Two conditions were set up; in one condition, the estimator slowly but surely started to overestimate. In the other condition, the estimator guessed accurately at first, then abruptly started to overestimate. Even though the eventual overestimates were the same, in the first "slippery slope" case, 52% of auditors went along with it, but under the second abrupt change condition, only 24% approved.

It is all too easy for our moral compasses to be taken off course, not through some conscious act of deception, but because we lose perspective and get drawn into an established way of seeing things without stepping back and seeing things through fresh eyes. Feedback should be the answer, but all too often, feedback givers' eyes are as clouded as our own. So if the standard approach to feedback isn't the answer, what is?

Getting Feedback Right

Successful leaders can't simply follow a formula and expect it to work – they need to fine-tune and adjust all the time – and so some form of feedback is clearly needed. However, I don't think that the well-embedded solutions of 360-degree, NPS or engagement surveys are doing the trick. They may have some place, but in addition, we need to attend to some simple, additional approaches.

- Use words, not numbers.
- Vary the methods and sources of feedback.
- Focus on outcomes, not just impressions.
- Observe, instead of relying on being observed.
- Don't rely on intermediaries.
- Embrace contradictions.
- Be informed by feedback, not led by it.

Let's take some time now to explore each of these.

Words Not Numbers

What is this obsession that we have with turning everything into a number? Maybe it is because the financial performance of a business is so easily expressed in numbers that we feel it is necessary to put other things in the same form if they are to hope to compete with cold, hard cash. If this is the case, then as an approach, it is counterproductive, as often the power of an insight is diminished by reducing it to a number. Think about it, what is more powerful – hearing that an IT system had a 0.1% downtime or hearing that the whole office had to stay late on a Friday afternoon? Do you listen more when you hear that your leadership rating is 4.5 out of 5, or that Julia is eternally gratefully for the sympathetic way you handled her recent bereavement? The words behind the numbers are so much more powerful, it amazes me that we are willing to forego them in favour of a leadership index.

Sure, numbers have advantages – they are quick and easy to read, you can track trends, and you can make comparisons between people – but all too often, they don't tell you what is really going on. In fairness, by focussing on the words, not just the numbers, it will take more time and be open to interpretation, but the benefits and insight that you gain are worth it. If you don't take this time for the words and instead build your business and leadership around metrics and indices, you are probably flying blind but falsely believing that the numbers are giving you sight.

Mix It Up

We have a tendency to settle in on a good feedback methodology and stick to it for a couple of really good reasons. Firstly, it is hard to find a good methodology in the first place, so we are reluctant to shift. Secondly, sticking to the same approach helps us to track the trends. This is all well and good, but unfortunately, it also leaves us susceptible to believing that our chosen perspective is the only perspective. I urge you to mix things up on a regular basis. Ask completely different people, completely different questions in a new way, and you will be surprised how many of the fixed opinions you have developed through pursuing your usual method are suddenly shattered.

Outcomes Not Impressions

Much feedback that we receive and rely on is based on what people think of us. We ask customers and staff to rate us against our chosen framework. We then treat these opinions as our feedback, but there are lots of other types of data that we track and measure in business that we could also regard as a form of feedback. For example, the sickness rate of my people is probably a better indication of my leadership than what they say about me in the survey.

We need to take great care to think about what we are really trying to achieve as leaders and identify the data that will tell us how we are actually doing and not just how people *think* we are doing. Feedback-givers are surprisingly inaccurate, even about themselves. I am reminded of a workshop that I was once involved in with a large organisation that produced many dominant brands. As part of the module on customer insight, participants were brought in a pile of customers' surveys that they read to understand which of their own brands would be most enjoyed by each customer. The participants felt that they had a good understanding of these customers and which products they would buy, so then came the big reveal. We had the actual customers who had filled in the forms in the next room. The participants now had the chance to speak with each of them and get some of that qualitative feedback. An hour later, we brought them back together and everyone spoke about how wrong they had been when they just looked at the numbers, and how speaking with the people had changed their minds about which products they would buy. So far so good, but now we did the second big reveal; we brought the customers back in and took them all to the supermarket to see how they actually behaved. It turned out that, while the numbers they had written were different to the words they spoke, the way that they actually behaved was different again. It was only by seeing how they actually behaved that we really understood the customer perspective.

Observe, Don't Rely On Being Observed.

A lot of the feedback that we receive is predicated on the assumption that certain groups of people are observing what we are doing and are then in a position to offer us feedback. While this may be true, I believe that we can gain even more feedback by being good observers ourselves. Let's say a leader wanted to know how engaging they were being in a meeting. He or she could ask people for their feedback at the end. If they did so, they would probably receive a blandly positive response. As an alternative, I will often suggest to my coachees that they do the observing instead. I encourage them to notice the impact that they are having in the room. Are people looking bored? Are they building on your ideas? After the meeting, are they still discussing the issue? It is actually quite remarkable how much feedback you can generate for yourself simply by looking and listening to the impact you are having.

Don't Rely On Intermediaries

The collection of feedback is an industry in its own right; whether it be outsourced to external consultancies or whether a team of people within the business make it their mission, there are plenty of people out there who are willing to give you help when it comes to feedback. For the busy executive, it is all too easy to rely on these intermediaries. People will do the hard slog of collecting feedback and then packaging and presenting it to you in bite-sized chunks. Let's face it, we don't necessarily enjoy getting feedback, so having someone who will push it to you on a regular basis ensures that it becomes a regular and disciplined part of life. The problem comes when we become so satisfied with the data that we are getting that we begin to rely on these intermediaries. Soon, we are never hearing what people actually think; we are hearing someone else's summary of what people think. That someone else may have a job they want to keep or a consulting contract that they can't afford to lose. They may have their own world view that they like to fit the feedback to match. They may believe that numbers are more powerful than words. They may be sensitive to your lack of time so filter out the noise. Whatever the case, a feedback system that comes through intermediaries has risk associated with it. So it is important to get back to the front-line and hear for yourself.

Embrace Contradictions.

Now there is a problem with going back to the front-line staff and hearing from them for yourself, and that is that everyone you see will tell you something different. They will all have their own personal hobbyhorses and will try to influence your opinion. If you gather lots of feedback from individuals, people are bound to disagree with each other. In response, leaders often say that they don't want to get bogged down in hearing a subset of issues from limited sources. That is why they need intermediaries to aggregate feedback from the whole business. To me, that is too easy a cop-out. OK, you can't go and visit every store or production line in your business, but I have rarely met a leader who didn't learn something valuable from the times that they did.

When you gather feedback broadly from the front-line, you will inevitably discover a high level of disagreement between people. Some will love your strategy and some will hate it. Some will think you are too hard and others, that you are too soft. This confusion can lead you to dismiss the feedback you are receiving as bias and opinion, and so perhaps dismiss the whole lot and return to the safety of metrics. However, if you persevere, you will develop a much richer sense of the complexity within your business. You will see how many of your decisions are tightropes that must carefully be walked. You will see that there are no simple answers that the gurus so readily want to sell us and, in doing so, you will increase your ability to find the right balance for your business.

Of course, the other possible explanation for the inconsistency of the feedback you are receiving is that you are showing inconsistent behaviour. This is all too common, as we do not always treat every person and every situation the same way. Once again, just because the feedback is inconsistent, it doesn't mean it is wrong.

Be Informed By Feedback Not Led By It

Success doesn't mean that everyone thinks you are great. A 100% approval rating does not mean victory, indeed, "Woe to you when all people speak well of you." The important thing is to understand the differences and decide for yourself whether they are differences with which you can live. Resist the temptation to be like a political party that is dictated to by focus groups and opinion pollsters. Leadership requires the making of difficult decisions that will not be approved of by everyone. Good feedback gives us a vivid sense of what those disagreements might be and why, but then its purpose is served and the rest is down to you.

Conclusion

So far in this book, we have seen the many reasons that the management gurus and other writers keep getting it wrong when they take success stories and turn them into panaceas. We have seen how a false assumption about cause and effect means that they may never succeed in their endeavour, and that the very seeking of success may in itself be too modest a goal for a leader of character. As there are no simple solutions, we must be adaptive learners who understand our own strengths and weaknesses, but then fine-tune them through effective feedback. Having said all of this, I would be reticent to lose some of the amazing learning that could emerge from the study of others and the thinking of leadership gurus and consultants. The problem is knowing which insight to keep and which to discard. I will give my own views of this in the final chapter, but before doing so, there is one last factor that needs to be considered when reading about leadership.

Every leader will surely encounter teachers, consultants and advisors who may offer them help in their business. Some of this help will be invaluable and some of it may even do you harm, and it is really difficult to differentiate between the two. While not a magic bullet, in judging your external sources of advice, it is very important to understand the business model behind any advice-giver. Bluntly, how are they hoping to make money out of you? You need to understand the financial imperatives that are behind every word that is being spoken to you. Understanding this gives you the final piece in the jigsaw and is the topic of the next chapter.

References

Gino, F. (2013) *Sidetracked: Why Decisions Get Derailed, And How We Can Stick To Plan*

Chapter 9
Show Me The Money:
Solutions Sell

"It's far more profitable to sell advice than to take it."
Steve Forbes

"I'm getting paid to write this book, and we all know that money distorts truth like a hippo in a thong."
Scott Adams

World Class Manufacturing

Around the same time that I was being wowed by my first guru, Tom Peters, one of the most notorious tales of the consulting industry was unfolding. Over in Ohio, Figgie International was a well-established manufacturing conglomerate with businesses as diverse as Rawling Sporting Goods and Scott Aviation. However, their attempt to implement "world-class manufacturing" across the business with the help of an army of consultants brought the company to its knees. The story is vividly told in the controversial 1997 bestseller by James O'Shea about the darker side of the consulting industry – *Dangerous Company*. Despite the huge criticism that it received from the consulting industry, to the non-consultant, it is a sobering perspective.

"The consultants produced high-priced reports about world-class manufacturing, one of those buzzwords that captured corporate imaginations. Instead of a world-class operation, though, Figgie would get a world-class mess. A lifetime of hard work would unravel before his eyes as the company Figgie cherished became a tale of consultants run amok. Eventually Figgie International would flirt with bankruptcy, its workforce would plunge into chaos, and its balance sheet would drown in red ink. Thousands of Figgie employees would lose their jobs in a wrenching downsizing that would leave the company prostate."

The company had certainly been in need of reform, and work in Clarke Reliance, another business owned by the Figgie family, had suggested a possible solution. It hadn't been cheap or easy, but with the help of some consultants from Deloitte and Touche, Clark Reliance appeared to have turned a corner and modernised. They achieved this feat by implementing what they called "world-class manufacturing". Exactly what this term meant was quite hard to define or quantify, but one of the consultants, Craig Giffi, had literally written the book about it.

"Published in 1990, by Dow Jones Irwin, *Competing in World-Class Manufacturing* drew a narrow audience and few reviews. Deloitte purchased a bunch of copies, though, and handed them out to clients, including the people at Figgie. It was a great marketing gimmick for the firm."

The decision to roll these ideas out to the rest of Figgie international required a huge number of consultants and a great deal of expensive, new equipment. The true details of what followed are in dispute. Was it poor consulting or poor management? Both sides clearly have their view, but according to *Dangerous Company* authors, James O'Shea and Charles Madigan, the results were clear.

"Despite spending more than $75 million for advice, it had barely escaped bankruptcy in 1994. Sales of $1.3 billion in 1989 had plunged to $319 million in 1994; profits of $63 million had turned into losses of $166 million. Instead of 17,000 employees, Figgie's workforce had plummeted to just 6,000."

The Leadership Industry

It seems that a good book idea and an army of consultants is a great way to make a whole bunch of money, even if it doesn't do the company who is paying it much good. In truth though, Figgie is often cited due to the extraordinary scale of the failure, and one must assume that the consultancy industry wouldn't have reached its current scale if every assignment had turned out like Figgie. And the scale of the industry really is huge. I have tried to get an accurate figure, but every source seems to disagree, although I can say with some certainty that the total consultancy market is likely to be worth hundreds of billion dollars. Much of this revenue comes from the world of IT consulting, but the "Leadership" part of it isn't to be sneezed at. Certainly, it is a subject that is written about a lot. According to Morris et al (2005), there were almost 400,000 articles and books on leadership at that time. While Barbara Kellerman in *The End of Leadership* quotes a more modest, but still impressive, trend: "In the early 1980s, an average of three books on leadership were published each year; by the end of the decade, that number was 23."

The books themselves are only part of the story; the real money seems to come from what happens next.

> "Reports from the training industry say that nearly $50 billion is spent annually on corporate training and development." (Gomez, 2007)

With so much money at stake, you can imagine that businesses in this industry have become pretty sophisticated at finding ways of securing their slice of this pie, year after year. When you read management theories and guru books, it is important to remember that, far from being standalone pieces of insight or theory, they are an integral part of a fiercely competitive industry. Even if it not obvious at first glance, there is a profit motive associated with nearly everything that you will ever read on the subject of leadership. I don't think that this is necessarily a bad thing, but given money's ability to "distort the truth like a hippo in a thong", it is vital to understand **how** the idea that you are reading about fits in with the industry as a whole.

If you understand that, you at least have some way of determining what sort of distortion there may be. So before we go further, this chapter will explain how books make money in this industry.

How Books Make Money

While there may be exceptions, I think that it is best to assume that making money is in some way associated with the publication of every leadership theory, model or book. True, people may say that they are writing their thoughts out of a love of the subject, a desire to add to the island of knowledge, or in an effort to make the world a better place. These are noble reasons to write and theorise, and certainly part of the story for most people. However, it would be naïve to assume that it is the whole story. Somewhere along the line, there is also profit to be had. That profit-making can come in many forms, but its existence can sometimes distort the content of books. It is therefore important to understand how money is made from the writing about leadership theories in order to be alert to any biases that may ensue.

There are four broad ways in which money can be made out of a leadership book. First, and most obviously, you can make money out of selling the actual copies of the book. Secondly, there is profit to be had in selling the time of the author of the book. Thirdly, consultancy (performed by people other than the author) can be sold to great profit. And finally, tools and instruments can be sold in vast numbers off the back of the right management theory. Let's take each of these four in turn to see how it works and determine how it may bias the content of a leadership book. At the end, I will tell you which of them applies to this book.

Selling Copies

The first, and most obvious, way to make money out of leadership books is selling them, but it would be a big mistake to make the assumption that this is the norm. Many writers in this field will buy more copies themselves to give away free to potential clients than they will sell on the open market. While there have been some amazing bestsellers in this space that have made a lot of money for the authors, that is far from the norm. Every writer may hope to be the next Malcolm Gladwell in the same way that many people want to win the lottery, but it would be foolish to plan your pension around such a rare occurrence. Every week that I have been writing this book, I have read the non-fiction bestseller league table in my national newspaper in an attempt to figure out what might sell. What I discovered was interesting and sobering; nearly every book on this list, week after week, was either by or about someone I had already heard of. It would seem that writing a book is a great way to make money from the fame that you already have, but an unknown writer is rarely likely to top the list.

In general, the bestselling leadership books have a similar formula; a hugely famous and successful business leader reveals "the secret of my success". If you are famous enough, you can do this many times over. Consider Richard Branson; at a recent bookstore,

I came across a whole shelf of books written by him about his approach. There was *Losing My Virginity; Screw It, Let's Do It: Lessons in Life; Like a Virgin: Secrets They Won't Teach You in Business School; The Virgin Way: How to Listen Learn, Laugh and Lead; Business Stripped Bare: Adventures of a Global Entrepreneur* and *Screw Business as Usual.* He even has his own publishing business to carry this material – Virgin Books. These books are clearly very popular as people are genuinely fascinated by such stories. I have already covered in earlier chapters why such reflections on the reasons for your own success are rarely accurate or useful, but at least we know what the writer is selling. Should you want to get a bit closer to the truth, you also have the option of reading a book *about* the famous leader in question from a more sceptical observer. For example, reading Tom Bower's *Branson: Behind the Mask* will give you a very different take on the man than ever appears in his own writing.

So, if you are already famous, there is likely to be a good market for books by or about you. If you want it to do really well, it needs to be entertaining and sell a good story, but it doesn't need to be that accurate or useful. Reputation management will clearly be important to anyone in the public eye, so don't expect much self-criticism. On the other hand, if you are reading an unauthorised biography then the opposite might apply, as dishing the dirt is always a winner. In short, if the main way of monetising a book is the selling of copies, expect the entertainment value to be higher than the utility or accuracy.

Selling Themselves

As it takes fame to guarantee the selling of many copies, then it should come as no surprise to find that building a personal brand and reputation is a main concern for a lot of other writers. Once you have made a name for yourself as a thinker in this space then a whole lot of other commercial opportunities open up. This category of money-making is probably the most benign, as it depends on the writer having something genuinely insightful or useful to say. The author can then sell more copies, speak publicly for a fee, or offer themselves up for personal consulting. Such an approach is stunningly lucrative. I was recently with the CEO of a very large UK business. He told me that he was just about to take his team off to the US to spend time with one of the famous writers named in this book. The fee for this private audience – a jaw-dropping $60,000. This fee only included a few hours with the great man himself.

How can these super-consultants charge such mammoth fees? Well one of the reasons must be that the buyer feels that the writer in question has some great, unique insight that will make all the difference. Alternatively, they may present some more obvious truth, but the CEO in question feels that hearing the same story from the mouth of such an esteemed thinker will give it more weight and so may help prompt action in the business. A little bit of stardust to sprinkle on the leadership team.

Anyone who expects leaders to fly around the world to hear them speak, and pay handsomely for the privilege, had better have something to say. There is therefore a need to have a powerful answer that will transform a business. It probably needs to be quite holistic and all-embracing. "I have figured out this little bit, but the rest still has me stumped" is not the best sales pitch for the aspiring guru, even if it is the reality in most situations. It is much better to say that you are confident that your super-theory is the answer to every question that any leader might have. Don't get me wrong, I gather that the CEO in question and his team had a very good experience on their trip and learned some things along the way. I wouldn't mind betting that the author has great consulting skills and the knowledge gained from working with so many businesses around the world has truly given him something worth sharing. They probably feel that it was $60k well spent. As I said, this is the most benign profit motive.

If this is the main way in which a book is going to lead to profit, it helps us to spot the potential for distortion and be duly sceptical. If you are reading one of these, you should be wary of stories that tell of how well the author has intervened with a client and transformed the business. You should watch out for the times that the author suggests, "all business would benefit from…" or similar generalisations. Finally, it is worth watching out for the latest thinking from someone who has had a big idea in the past. This is actually a very tough one to call, as it could go either way. On the one hand, a writer who has achieved a breakthrough and sold millions of copies on their theory will be invited in to meet some of the most influential people in the world; they will learn a lot and so reading whatever they write next may help you share in some of that insight, and it is likely that a great thinker will keep being a great thinker. On the other hand, there is a risk of something less helpful.

Imagine you have discovered an amazing approach to improving business. For a couple of years, you make your living off it, but eventually, people move on. If you are to keep the money rolling in, you are going to have to say something new. Even if you don't have anything new to say, the only advice that I can give is to judge each new idea on its own merits.

Despite the high fees, you won't really enter the big leagues just by selling your own time. In fact, even the previously-mentioned $60k had to be shared. The UK leadership team that I mentioned actually spent two days with the guru's "team" and only a few hours with the man himself. If you really want to multiply your earnings, you need to find a way of selling the time of other people too. You enter the world of selling consulting.

Selling Consulting

So you have made a name for yourself and customers are beating a path to your door, but there are only so many hours in a day, so it makes sense to introduce these clients to a colleague who can do just as good as a job as yourself in applying your ideas in their business, right? You take a cut of the cash for introducing the colleague and everyone is happy. Well yes, in theory, but there is a big problem. Experienced consultants cost money. If your colleague really is as effective as you are, then fairly soon she will expect to get pretty much all the money or else she will take her talents elsewhere. The trick to making a fortune in consulting is being able to pass on lots of work to much cheaper consultants, leaving more of the margin to you. Naturally, if the consultant is cheaper, then they are also likely to be less experienced. You therefore need to find a way to ensure that your big idea can be implemented by more junior people – preferably by lots of them. What you need is a good model or simple process that you can teach to your junior consultants and have them roll out, just like in the Figgie example.

Unfortunately, if the model is simple, then pretty soon, clients will also develop the same competence and not need you, so on a regular basis, you might want to introduce a new model or an update to the old, to keep clients dependent on your small army. Alternatively, you can make the methodology so time-consuming to implement that your own staff won't have the capacity. The consultants may even try to build many of your business systems on their model, making it very hard for you to move away from their approach and, heaven forbid, think for yourself. Now I am not saying that models are a bad thing in themselves; they can help people to get their head around complex ideas. However, it is really worth understanding whether the book that you are reading is showing you a model just to be helpful or whether it is part of a consulting offering. Do *you* really need a new way of looking at your business or is it the consultancy's need that is being met.

Likewise, while there are clearly some initiatives that may benefit from bringing in additional people for a short period of team, it is worth questioning whether any business solution that appears to require it is doing so for the right reasons. Is it the best way to change your business or just the best way for a consultancy to profit?

It is not just the consultancies that have the knack of selling on to cheaper resources; academic institutions can get more leverage from their star names too. Big name thinkers enhance the reputation of an entire institution and may attract students, but not all the teaching needs to be delivered by the star of the show. Even short executive courses can command high fees. For example, Wharton's two-week Executive Development Program is listed as costing $26k per person.

Selling Tools

A nice model that can be rolled out through cheap, young consultants is all well and good, but even that doesn't fully leverage your big idea. It is still limited by the need for people to act as intermediaries. What you really need in order to make money while you sleep is a good tool. An online course, an app or a psychometric instrument can be sold in very high volumes and, with no pesky consultants to pay, it is pretty much all profit. Now if your book suggests that all companies are different and require bespoke solutions, then that does you no good at all when it comes to selling a tool. What you really need to do is conclude that your "5 Leadership Essentials" or "7 Organisational Competencies" are universally applicable, and so can be turned into a neatly replicable tool. You can then even sell the ability to benchmark yourself against other companies or leaders. This may be fine and exactly what your business needs, but you really do need to understand that this is what is going on in the background when reading about the next big thing that an author is selling you.

There is one fact about consulting that consultants are somewhat loath to admit – the person doing the consulting is the most important component. As with many walks of life, the practitioner is often more important than the tools that they use. If I am going to select a builder to renovate my house, I won't spend much time worrying about how big his drill is. Instead, I will look at the work he has done before and hear from previous customers. Likewise, when you work with a consultant, the actual skills and experience of the individual that you are working with is more important than the tool that they are using. However, because the best consultants cost a lot of money, many firms will prefer you to focus on the quality of their tool or method and provide reams of statistics about their methodology to draw your attention away from the cheap junior consultants who will eventually implement it. The blunt truth is that a great leader or consultant can do amazing things with the simplest of methodologies, but an incompetent fool won't be rescued by the latest business model.

In my field of business psychology, the tool of choice is the psychometric test. These can be really useful, and I will often use one of them myself. It is also a big industry; my former colleague, Nik Kinley (2013), estimated it at $2-4 billion per year. As you might expect, there are a great many articles and books that have been written about these psychometrics, but in reading these texts, I also need to be aware of who is writing them. I am sure that it will not surprise you to learn that huge numbers of articles, books and papers extolling the virtues of a particular psychometric just happen to be written by an employee of the company that sells it. It will surprise you even less to learn that the writers in question rarely conclude that the test they are examining is ineffective.

These issues were really brought home to me in Robert Forde's 2015 paper, *When Profit Comes In The Door, Does Science Go Out The Window?* In it, he says:

> "One example is the Myers-Briggs Type Indicator (MBTI), which is still widely used, especially in the occupational field. According to its publisher's website, it is used in over two million assessments annually and is the most popular personality assessment in the world... The website mentions some of the more favourable results, but not the fact that Myers and Briggs were qualified neither in psychology nor in test development. It also mentions that the company has been responsible for developing and marketing the MBTI since 1975, but not that it was previously published by the Educational Testing Service, which withdrew it after an internal report on its accuracy and psychometric properties."

Personal Declaration Of Profit Motive

In the next, and final, chapter, I am going to lay out for you my own approach to leadership, informed by decades of experience as both a consultant and a business leader myself, and also by the insights that I have laid out in this book. It is therefore only right and proper that you should be asking yourself what my profit motive is. I can hardly encourage you to be sceptical about management writers without also applying that same scepticism to me. So which of the four options is the way in which I am trying to profit from the writing of this book? I could of course claim that I am only doing it out of the goodness of my heart and for the betterment of humankind, but if you believe that is all there is to it then go to the back of the class and read the whole book again.

To answer the question of personal motive, I need to give you some context on myself. Having started my career in the world of telecoms and something called Human-Computer Interaction, since 1994, I have spent my life in the world of consulting (so that should make you suspicious for a start). However, after 17 years with one particular consultancy, I have made the huge step of going "in-house" and I am currently working once again in telecoms. This has given me a unique opportunity to step away from consultancy and view it with a dispassionate eye, and without the need to sell a particular profit or service. However, I have my future career to think about and may well find myself back in consulting once again. Because of this, I am firmly in the "selling themself" category. I am not realistically going to be making a fortune "selling copies", as I am not famous and I don't currently have any consultancy or tools to sell. However, I would be delighted if this book led some readers to feel that they wanted to meet and work with me in the future. Beware, however, just because I am not a consultant at the moment, it doesn't mean I don't think like one. So stay alert for overly simple answers in this book.

If you accept that my main motivation for writing this book is selling myself, you are better able to spot the parts of my writing to take with a pinch of salt. I would urge you to keep a special eye out for times when I:

- Imply that I know or can do something that nobody else can
- Name-drop
- Make myself look good

Let me now give you another personal declaration. A major motivation for writing this book has been to clarify in my own mind the things that I have learned from years of experience, to express the frustrations I have felt at overly simple solutions that just don't work, and to provide something that will be useful to leaders, their businesses and customers. As such, please stay with me for one last chapter as I try to distil it all into a new philosophy of leadership.

References

Forde, Robert (2015) *When Profit Comes In The Door, Does Science Go Out The Window? Assessment and Development Matters, Vol.7 No. 1, Spring 2015*

Giffi, C. (1990) *Competing in World Class Manufacturing*

Gomez, D. (2007) *The Leader as Learner, International Journal of Leadership Studies 2, No 3*

Kellerman, B. (2012) *The End of Leadership*

Kinley, N. and Ben-Hur, S. (2013) *Talent Intelligence: What you need to know to identify and measure talent*

Morris, J. A., Brotheridge, C. M. and Urbanski, J. C. (2005) *Bringing Humility To Leadership: Antecedents And Consequences Of Leader Humility, Human Relations, 58*, pp 1323-50

O'Shea, J. and Madigan, C. (1997) *Dangerous Company: Management Consultants and the Businesses They Save and Ruin*

Chapter 10
No More Heroes Anymore:
The Red Pill Leader Is Revealed

"Show me a hero and I'll write you a tragedy."
F. Scott Fitzgerald

Hero Worship

Throughout my childhood, my mother dedicated her life to children with cerebral palsy. She was a nursery teacher in a school that helped and educated those with this and other severe conditions. As is this case with many such institutions, her school was backed by a charity and was in need of frequent fundraising activities. Summertime would always bring about a host of fetes and fairs and, if the school was lucky, a celebrity visit would be arranged to draw in the crowds. One year was particularly memorable – it was 1979, The International Year of the Child. As such, we knew we had a special visitor for the fete that took place in the grounds that surrounded the school. My mother's classroom opened onto the back lot of the school, where various stalls were arranged and we waited with anticipation for a big TV celebrity to appear. We had learned that he was taking the time to stop at each and every stall, thank the volunteers for their support and buy something from them. We were really hoping that something similar would happen for us. Soon, we could hear the noise of the great man coming around the corner, pursued by a horde of shouting children who were clamouring for an autograph. Besieged by his fans, he stopped abruptly outside of our room and, with great authority, commandeered a table and chair to set up an impromptu autograph signing desk. I couldn't believe my luck. The table was set up with its back to the classroom, such that I found myself stood next to his seat while everyone else was kept on the other side of the desk.

Time stood still for me; I have no real sense of how long he sat there, chatting with children – I was simply enthralled by his presence. For years afterwards, my mother would laugh as she retold the story of how I stood rooted to the spot, with my mouth open, watching him play the crowd like an orchestra. I have never before or since seen such charisma and interpersonal power. It was like watching some irresistible force of nature. It was only decades later, after his death, that this man was exposed as the most notorious and prolific child sex offender in UK history. The name Jimmy Savile now sends a shudder down the spine of anyone like me who grew up in the 1970s. He had systematically used his fame, charitable work and close association with many schools and institutions for vulnerable children to abuse those who were most needing of protection. His fame and hero status protected him in a way that we now find hard to believe.

Leader Heroes

Throughout this book, there has been the recurrent theme of the leadership or business hero, but over and again, we have seen how the desire for a perfect hero can be thwarted. The role model CEOs in one management book see their reputation tarnished a few years later. For a while, I thought that the only way for someone to stay a hero was to die a hero, but even that may not be the case. Reputations can be tarnished even after death.

Having interviewed about 2,000 senior leaders over my career, I am in no doubt that there are brilliant leaders out there and there are also terrible ones. However, it is hard to say, "Behave exactly like this and you too will succeed", as so much is dependent on luck and context. Even those brilliant leaders that I have seen can easily find themselves in the wrong business in the future and then fail. So, now I invite you to take the red pill. Instead of seeking a neat solution or formula for business success, I will invite you to face the reality of business life. Within it, you will find contradictions and imperfections. You will also find that, for most problems, there is no right answer and, even if you take the least bad option, you may still fail. However, I have noticed that the leaders that I admire most and fail the least do have some things in common. These things seem to maximise their chances of success. Nothing is guaranteed, but in this final chapter, I will lay out the orientation and approach that I have seen succeed most often.

Tightropes To Be Walked

We have previously considered the role of positive visualisation in athletes. On the one hand, it is useful to visualise your own success and have no doubt that you will win. On the other hand, everyone else is doing the same thing, so as most sports have many more competitors than winners, you are still more likely to lose than win. Having lost, you must figure out what you can learn from the failure and still believe that visualising success will work next time. A capacity to accept such fundamental contradictions, and indeed embrace them, is a success trait in its own right. It is not enough to say that these competing factors must be in balance, so I will visualise success but with a reasonable expectation that it won't work, even though that is truer. No, you must totally believe in success and totally face up to failure. Within leadership, there are a range of other, similar, tensions.

The essence of leadership success is to know what contradictory and opposing forces one needs to manage and to walk a tightrope between them. This tightrope walking does not mean attending to both forces a bit; rather it means attending to both forces totally and wholeheartedly, even though they contradict one another. Sometimes, the context will mean that you need to lean in one direction more strongly for a while, and sometimes, you will need to lean the other way. The secret is to neither favour left nor right, but rather to have a good sense of balance and permanently adjust as one crosses the ravine.

For many years, like a lot of people, I railed against the inconsistent leaders who were above me. "Last week, you said one thing, and this week, you are saying the opposite," I would complain. By contrast, on first glance, it looked more admirable to see the leader who made a decision and stuck with it, come what may. Over time, however, I noticed that the inconsistent leaders often did better than the ones that stuck solidly to their approach. For a while, I worked for someone who repeatedly said, "We are a premium brand, we must not discount; we must hold our nerve." Then, to the dismay of several account managers who had lost business because of this policy, he abruptly started discounting. To some degree, I joined the grumbling. "Why aren't we more clear about our strategy and stick to it?" we said. A few years later, I found myself the leader of a similar business and surprised myself by doing exactly the same thing. Striving to be the premium brand was important, but so was making payroll. We were in danger of toppling off the tightrope and I had to make a quick adjustment. Fortunately, I had great followers who confronted me with my inconsistency, so I learned to explain the reasons for the adjustments that I was making. This meant that they could tell a fundamental change of strategy from a forced, pragmatic compromise.

There appeared to me to be three particularly important tightropes that need to be walked simultaneously by a leader, and I will spend the chapter exploring each of them. I do not claim that this is an exhaustive list, and so welcome any additions to it. Each tightrope is expressed by a pair of important, but often contradictory, forces.

1. Values Preservation versus Value Creation
2. Push versus Pull
3. Strategic Thinking versus Operational Delivery

Values Preservation Versus Value Creation

This tightrope, in most cases, boils down to the tension between doing what we think is right (Values Preservation) and making money (Value Creation). Recently, a whole range of people have argued that these things are not in tension at all, but rather that ethical leadership, employee and customer focus all lead to business success. Overall, in the long-run, these people may well be right. However, "in the long-run" may mean long after the leader making the critical decisions has left. On a day-to-day basis, we may be faced with less high-minded businesses practices that give competitors an advantage and may put our own profit in peril. We see valueless leaders floating away on golden parachutes and leaving others to pick up the mess. We see noble people having business disasters. It is naïve to assume that following Aristotle's ideal to "live life by a higher code" will also lead to business success. The easy compromise would be to adopt an approach of "we will try to be good, as long as it doesn't lose us money", but that is equally wrong, and just the start of a slippery slope. Instead, the leader must find a way to being fully committed to their values AND fully committed to business success, and that is much easier said than done.

So what are these values that must be balanced with profit? Beyond business ethics, they may include the real valuing of our employees, being truly customer-centric, treating suppliers fairly, or protecting the environment. I could make the case, and many have, that each one of these things leads to business success, so where is the conflict? However, anyone who has actually been on the front-line of a business knows that keeping your balance is exceptionally difficult. The truth is that behaving the way that you want for your employees, customers or whoever will initially cost some money – money that you may not have or may not have the licence to use. I have been with leaders who knew that their employees were overworked and suffering with stress, but found that the profitability of the business was dependent on keeping headcount down. Other businesses have confronted the fact that much of their profit comes from loyal customers paying higher rates than new ones. Retailers delight in offering low prices to their customers at the expense of suppliers. These same suppliers have then been all but destroyed by aggressive purchasing. Industries have treated environmental damage as a cost that only needs to be paid by future generations. Remedying these situations is not easy; they require exceptional courage, influencing skills and even luck.

What about when the challenge is in the other direction? Might there be leaders out there who focus too much on values protection and too little on value generation? Yes, there certainly are, and I have met a few in my time. They may resemble the award-winning leader that I mentioned in an earlier chapter, whose business had just gone bust, or they may find themselves struck and frustrated at middle levels of organisations that do not appreciate them, as failing to deliver financial value is quickly punished in the market. However, if you are, by preference, values first, then all is not lost, as commerciality can be learned and if you can crack both ends of the spectrum, you really do become a leader to be reckoned with.

Given the apparent business bias against values, the logic of rebalancing in their direction is obvious, but the practice of it is a genuine challenge. These dilemmas are real for many business leaders, and failing to name and acknowledge them does those leaders a disservice, as it pushes underground a debate that should see the light of day. I have seen leaders embrace both ends of the spectrum (values preservation and value creation), but I know that it is hard and that it takes courage and belief. It also requires honesty, feedback and conversation. Frequently, the leader will need to convince others (bosses, shareholders and the like) to face up to these contradictions. Yet a failure to discuss the tensions inherent in the effort effectively forces our tightrope walker to wear a blindfold too.

In *The Ten Golden Rules of Leadership: Classical Wisdom for Modern Leaders*, Michael Soupios and Panos Mourdoukoutas draw on Classical Greek literature for some business insight:

"Sophocles produced a play in 409 BC titled *Philoctetes*; a work we believe should be read and carefully considered by every executive. The two central characters in this drama are Neoptolemus and the famous hero of Troy, Odysseus. From the drama's outset, it is clear that the figures are juxtaposed, not simply as different personalities but as representatives of entirely distinct life orientations. Neoptolemus is the son of Heracles, perhaps the greatest of all Greek heroes. He is a young man of undefiled principle for whom honor and integrity are primary concerns of life. By contrast, Odysseus is a man famous for enchanting the souls of others with his wily words. In the ancient literature, he is often described as possessing metis, meaning "shrewdness" or "craftiness". It should be noted that this term does not imply wisdom or intellectual insight. On the contrary, metis suggests the guile and cunning of the fox. In short, Odysseus is a man of mischief and deceit, intent upon compromising the youthful integrity of Neoptolemus.

"Throughout the play, Odysseus advances a dishonourable agenda as old as humanity itself, that is cited just as often (perhaps more) today than it was in antiquity. It is the notion that the end justifies the means; that a person is entitled to engage in whatever conduct is necessary in order to accomplish his or her agenda. In other words, one should not allow moral concerns to impede the necessities of practical achievement. In response to this seductive reasoning, the young Neoptolemus responds, 'I would prefer even to fail with honor than win by cheating.'"

Now, if I was to fall off the tightrope one way then I would prefer it to be in Neoptolemus' direction, but I would rather not fall at all. The challenge then is to win with honour, and that means fully embracing the competing forces of values preservation and value creation.

You may have noticed, and indeed been frustrated by, my failure to provide an answer to this dilemma, but of course, that is the nature of a dilemma. However, I looked at overdone strengths in Chapter 7, and at feedback mechanisms in Chapter 8. If anything, they are the closest things that we have to a solution. If you are aware of the tightrope you are walking, and are determined to do so, then the next thing is to be aware of your own imbalance. If you were to fall, which way would it be? The next is to enhance your balance, and in the business world, that means having a rich source of feedback to replicate the balancing mechanisms of your inner ear. There is no easy answer; the wind may blow and you will have to adjust; enemies may shake the rope, but as long as you remember that you are on a tightrope, you might just stand half a chance of making it to the other side?

Finally, let's revisit the tightrope metaphor. It is easy to think of balance as coming from a little of both attributes. However, a much more stable balance comes from having a heavy weight on both sides (hence, the use of balancing poles). Having a lot of weight on both sides is advantageous. This translates into meaning that you have to have absolute and total commitment to values **and** an absolute and total commitment to value creation, even when they contradict each other.

Push Versus Pull

A great leader has a vision; she stands firm, is clear and decisive. A great leader is humble; she responds to feedback and adapts to changing circumstances. I believe both of these sentences are true, even though they appear to be describing two completely different people. Now, one could argue that they represent two different ways of leading, suited to different businesses, but I am not so sure. I don't know of any business that needs all of one, but none of the other. Every business that I have ever worked with needed both; in fact, it needed a lot of both. By the same token, any one leader, no matter how big or small, will, at times, need to focus on telling and at other times, asking and listening. Once again, this doesn't mean being some wishy-washy mixture of the two. It means fully being one sometimes and fully the other at other times. As a leader, can you be really strong and unbending when the circumstance demands, yet humble and flexible when those circumstances change? I sometimes think of these contrasting styles as "pushing" or "pulling". Let's look at them in more detail.

The Case For "Pushing"

Clarity really matters. What are we trying to achieve? How will we measure success? What will we prioritise? What are our values? What is our plan? What are my objectives? These and many other questions are asked in an attempt to provide the clarity that most people need. Clearly telling people what is expected from them is Management 101. SMART goals, management by objectives, vision setting, and straight feedback are all techniques that are in a successful leader's toolkit, and all of them require an individual to assert their point of view. Once the clarity is given, however, things won't often go according to plan. It is easy to be pulled in many different directions. Person after person will come to you with problems, exceptions or other priorities that can take you off-course, and it takes a true leader to stand firm, not wobble and keep the faith. The confidence of the leader can be infectious, and a team can be driven to achieve what they previously believed to be impossible goals.

There are lots of big characters around the typical leadership table. If you are not bold and confident to speak up, or if you do not have the right impact, your voice may not get heard. It is therefore important for a leader to have presence and impact. You will often need to argue their case with a stubborn determination. You will hear back lots of reasonable arguments, contended by forceful and eloquent colleagues, and it would be easy to be influenced by these arguments. However, listening to them can be the start of a slippery slope. Pretty soon, people will accuse you of swaying with the wind and being overly influenced by the latest person to get your ear. For this reason, I have often referred my coaches to a quote from George Bernard Shaw:

"The reasonable man adapts himself to the world; the unreasonable one persists in trying to adapt the world to himself. Therefore, all progress depends on the unreasonable man."

Actually, I kept this quote in my own bag too, as it was something that I struggled with personally.

When anyone came to me with a reasonable request, my desire to be nice and have people think well of me would lead me to say "yes", even if it was a bad use of my time. When I made requests of people, I would be sympathetic to their difficulties and often let them off. It took some time for me to cope with the emotional pressure that comes with being unreasonable. However, over and again I could see leaders achieving great success by being pushier than I felt comfortable being. I remember one executive chairman of a food manufacturer setting his UK head what we all believed was an impossible goal. There were two customers that mattered greatly to the business, but cooperating with one would greatly upset the other. "Which one do I let down?" asked the leader. "Neither," replied the executive chairman. "You will find a way of helping both of them without upsetting anyone." The leader shot back, "Honestly, it is impossible, <customer A> told me so." The chairman smiled. "And yet," he murmured, "that is exactly what you are going to do." After the meeting, the dumped-on leader vented to me about the unreasonableness of his boss. The funny thing was, a few months later, he found a way to do what was asked of him.

The blunt truth is that "pushy" leaders get stuff done, stubborn leaders persevere to the end, and decisive leaders are easier to follow. Unfortunately, this is only half the story, as somehow, you need to be the polar opposite too.

The Case For "Pulling"

As a leader, you only succeed through others, so having highly talented people on your side is crucial for anyone who runs a business. By and large, however, you don't get the best from brilliant people by telling them what to do all the time. You need to really listen to what they are telling you and make adaptions as necessary. History is littered with leaders too arrogant to heed the advice of their people, and who charged ahead into disaster. A leader with humility, who listens to feedback and is prepared to admit mistakes, is surely more likely to both avoid disaster and win the loyalty and respect of her people.

If you tune into the needs of others, rather than repeatedly sound off about your own, you will be able to connect your business imperatives to the motivations of others. Once you have done that, you won't need to drive your people on – they will take the initiative and do it themselves. A rigid tree that does not sway with the wind is much more likely to break. So, rather than being a weakness, the willingness to adapt is a source of great strength.

And what about persuasion and influence? Sure, the loud and forceful executive will get her voice heard and command the room, but will she really win people's hearts, or has she just beaten them into submission? Surely her colleague, who takes the time to listen and pull out the concerns of others, when she does reach agreement, does so in a deep and meaningful manner.

So where does this all lead us? Great leaders are pushy and unreasonable. They are also humble and understanding. Surely these things are opposite ends of a spectrum. How can anyone be both? To resolve this tension, many people opt for one style or the other, and while with that comes the danger that they are missing the benefits of the other approach, there are examples of both types of success story. Others try to find a safe middle ground; they are a little bit "pushy" and a little bit "pully", but by doing neither of them well, the impact is lost. The great paradox is that an excellent leader may well be the person who is world-class at being both ends of the spectrum at the same time. Well maybe not exactly the same time, but at the very least, on the same day. They need to spot the times to be utterly stubborn and unreasonable, and the times to shut up, listen and eat humble pie.

Strategic Thinking Versus Operational Delivery

You may well have noticed that there is a time horizon effect to the previous two "polarities". Values preservation has benefits that may take time to appear; meanwhile, those focussed on short-term value may have already driven you out of business. A "pulling" boss wins long-term loyalty, but a pushy one gets things done fast. A similar short-term versus long-term tension is at the heart of most debates of strategy versus operations, but I think that there is much more to it than that.

A company that I was at once received a visit from a noted senior executive in one of the world's biggest companies. As he mingled with our junior staff, he delighted in tormenting them with the question, "What is more important, strategy or execution?" They all squirmed with the difficulty of picking one over the other, as clearly both matter. Whether you frame it as thinking versus doing, direction versus delivery, or destination versus journey, we seem to find it hard to attend to both things at once. It is not enough to simply put your head down and strive for excellence; leaders must keep a keen eye on market trends and competitors, and then place big bets as to what to do in the future. On the other hand, no amount of strategic brilliance will save your company if you can't turn plans into reality and get stuff done.

One of the most amazing leaders that I have worked with is John Forrest. He was the COO of Premier Inn, a hotel chain that came to dominate the industry in the UK with its ability to consistently deliver a great night's sleep and competitive prices. During his tenure, John took the chain from 450 to 701 hotels; that is from 32,600 to 60,000 rooms. Each and every one of those rooms need to be spotless, have comfortable beds, be quiet, have internet connection, and a whole host of other things. Delivering that attention to detail, day after day, on an industrial scale, is no mean feat. John immersed himself totally and personally in this endeavour. He would attend each and every hotel opening and was only stopped from this when growth accelerated to the degree that more than one hotel would open at the same time, and even he couldn't be in two places at once. One of his mantras is, "What you permit, you promote." By this, he means that if, as a leader, you walk by the smallest impediment to a great customer experience, you are effectively signalling to all your followers that letting the customer down in that way is fine, and pretty soon, your organisation will be rife with it. He does it with charm, a smile and gratitude for the hard work of his people, but he always stops to put even the smallest detail right. Some leaders think that they are running the business when they examine charts and spreadsheets – they are content with their high-level dashboards – but John knows that what really matters is the experience of every customer in every room, and he dedicates his life to getting that right.

On the other hand, it is easy for competitors to start to copy successful formulas and, pretty soon, you are under price pressure as more and more businesses compete for the same dollar. Like sharks in a feeding frenzy, the ocean soon fills with blood. You find yourself in what W. Chan Kim and Renee Mauborgne call a Red Ocean. It takes real strategic innovation to move your business out into a new patch of Blue Ocean.

It would be easy to say that you must do both – you must have John's operational obsession, while also finding patches of Blue Ocean – but the reality is actually quite challenging. Imagine this very real dilemma that I have seen played out in a boardroom. You and your biggest competitor have both decided to open up for business in the same new town. However, it seems that this town just isn't big enough for both of you. Month after month, the sales figures roll in, and you are making a loss; intelligence suggests that your competitor is too. You decide to discount your way to victory and your competitor responds. Now you are both losing even more money. You could close down a clearly underperforming business; this would improve your overall business profitability, but it would help your competitor even more. The strategic move might be to close it anyway and concentrate on other areas. Another strategic decision might be to assume that you will take the pain longer than them, and so eventually, the competitor will quit. Working out the best course of action is agonising and time-consuming. In the meantime, who has the spare bandwidth to attend to excellence in a seemingly simple and mundane world of delivering good products and service? Once again, the solution isn't to be a little bit strategic and a little bit operational. One must somehow be exceptional at both, despite the differences between them

Other Tightropes To Be Walked

In this chapter, I have named what I see to be the three most important tightropes to be walked, but they are by no means the only ones. Each industry, each business and each leader may to figure their own ones. The issues where one cannot be either/or, the ones where one must be both/and, even if that creates a paradox. Here are some other options of polarities to consider, but feel free to add your own:

i.   *Preservation versus Innovation*: How do you protect you core – "stick to your knitting" and value your core competence – while at the same time, diversifying into new areas and inventing the future?

ii. *Simplicity versus Choice*: How do you focus on core products done brilliantly, while also creating a diverse enough offering to meet all customer needs?

iii. *Empowerment versus Control*: How do you give freedom to your front-line employees to serve the customer, while at the same time, defining uncompromising standards?

iv. *Optimism versus Pessimism*: How can you assume success and make a leap of faith, while also preparing for the worst and ensuring that you are stepping on firm ground?

v. *Culture Fit versus Diversity*: How do you create a cohesive culture and recruit people that fit it, while at the same time, embracing diversity and all the benefits that flow from that?

A Final Polarity

As I struggle to arrive at a conclusion that can take you forward as a leader, I realise that I am faced with my own dilemma, as two seemingly different paths are ahead and both may be true. On the one hand, I could argue that the truly great leader must be able to handle both ends of every spectrum simultaneously. On the other hand, I can think of countless examples of people who have clearly been skewed one way or another, and yet still succeeded. To make matters more complex, some people have tried to be both and have ended up wishy-washy and ineffectual in the middle, while others have prided themselves on being firmly at one end of the spectrum, yet have failed spectacularly as a result. As with everything in this book, once you have taken the red pill, you discover that there is no simple and easy answer that will apply to everyone. I suspect those that heed the advice of Chapter 8 (about strengths) and

Chapter 9 (about feedback) are more likely to succeed, but I can't prove it.

What I do know is that there is more than one path that can be taken. Those that claim that you **must** play dirty to win are wrong, but at the same time, those that say cheats never prosper are sadly also wrong. Those that excuse their excesses with claims that it is a dog eat dog world need to reconsider their morality, but those who think that being nice to everyone is all that is needed may have to prepare for bankruptcy. Those that pride themselves on pushiness number as many leaders as those that cherish their ability to listen. Being able to excel at both ends of each spectrum is clearly an ideal that some have mastered. Those who are not able to do so run real risks of suffering for their imbalance, but even those people may avoid disaster with the help of others.

So I am left with the one question that I think matters above all others. **What kind of leader do you want to be?** Do you wish to be the financially-driven, pushy operator? If you do, that's fine, but know that it is not the only way to succeed, and know the risks you run in doing so. Likewise, if you see yourself as the strategic, values-oriented and listening leader, that is fine too, but it doesn't make you superior or more likely to succeed. It also comes with significant risk. Whatever you decide, don't kid yourself that you have to be that way because it is the only way to succeed; rather accept that is a choice that you have made. Once you have figured out the leadership path that is right for you, be that leader brilliantly. That means understanding the real conflicts and paradoxes that exist in running any business and trying to manage them. Will this be a recipe for success? No. Can I guarantee you success? No, but you stand more chance of succeeding than you do by blindly following the advice of others. And, if you fail, at least you do so on your own terms.

My Own Red Pill

In addition to having been a consultant for many decades, I also slowly but surely found myself being a business leader in my own right. Like everyone else, I had my own imbalances, not least my reticence to push. I aspired to being the Values Preserving leader, but as commercial pressure built, I occasionally found myself flying to the other end of the spectrum, rather than excelling at both simultaneously. Those times hurt me spiritually and emotionally, and so eventually, I resolved to be the leader I wanted to be, regardless of the consequences. That decision led to what people who judge success based on power and money alone might have described as my biggest failure. However, when I look back at that experience, I have no regret for the "failure", but deep remorse for the times when I failed to be the leader that I wanted to be. In the next phase of my career, I discovered a context where I could be both true to myself and succeed. So if you are in a context where being true to yourself conflicts with success – leave, and go and find a context where you can.

Conclusion

We began this book by looking at the work of the great leadership gurus and discovered just how hard it was to predict the continual success of already-great companies, let alone transfer their lessons to your own business. We explored some of the reasons that gurus get it wrong. We saw that our love for stories inevitably means that we are following a simple narrative, rather than the complex truth. We discovered just how prevalent sudden failure may be. We learned to doubt the accuracy of the stories that we are told by compelling CEOs who may know less about the reason for their own success than they think (or at least write). We saw the damaging effect of fashions and the desire for the next big thing. We also faced the issue of statistics and the truth that they so often obscure.

In Chapter 7, we faced two more fundamental questions. Does simple cause and effect break down when you are leading a large and complex business? And should "success" really be the yardstick against which we measure everything?

So what do we do about all this? Well, I hope that the later chapters have given you some ideas – ideas about how to manage your strengths and weaknesses, and ideas about getting the most from feedback. Until finally, we arrive at the messy truth. Leadership involves contradictions, but the beauty of these contradictions is that there is more than one path that can be followed. You have the ability to be your own guru, to decide for yourself the leader that you wish to be and then be that person. If the context that you find yourself in doesn't seem to allow you to be your own ideal leader, then change the context. I know that it is possible to wrestle with these contradictions and win. I can't bottle the magic formula, as it is ever-changing but, having taken the red pill, I trust that you will find the way.

References

Kim, W. C. and Mauborgne, R. (2015) *Blue Ocean Strategy: How to Create Uncontested Market Space and Make the Competition Irrelevant*

Soupios M. A. and Mourdoukoutas, P. (2015) *The Ten Golden Rules of Leadership: Classical Wisdom for Modern Leaders*

Printed in Great Britain
by Amazon